Anarchism and the Body

Michelle M. Campbell

(Guest Editor)

CONTENTS

Anarchist Developments in Cultural Studies (ADCS) is an international, peer-reviewed, open-access journal devoted to the study of new and emerging perspectives in anarchist thought and practice from or through a cultural studies perspective. The interdisciplinary focus of the journal presumes an analysis of a broad range of cultural phenomena, the development of diverse methodological traditions, as well as the investigation of both macro-structural issues and the micro-logical practices of everyday life. ADCS is an attempt to bring anarchist thought into contact with innumerable points of connection.

Website:
www.Anarchist-Developments.org

ISSN: 1923-5615

ARTICLES

1.

Anarchism and the Body

Michelle M. Campbell*

"The question of souls is old—we demand our bodies, now"
Voltairine de Cleyre, [1914] (2016)

This special edition has its origin story in a conference held at Purdue University in the summer of 2015. Scholarly anarchism still retains a healthy DIY culture, and when I decided many months before that I wanted to get a group of scholars and activists together to talk about anarchism and bodies, all it took was a community and an intellectual hunger. Before I had gotten up the gall to organize a whole conference, I had long wondered: where is the body in our anarchist theory?, how do we account for it?, and how does it figure into our praxis?

A motley crew of activists and academics, many of whom consider themselves both, arrived in the heat of the Indiana summer ready to engage in both theory and praxis. The conference program was diverse both in content and approaches. Panels consisted of papers centered on structures of domination and liberation; anarchist publications and cultural artifacts; the laboring body and class organizing; "troubled" reproductions; art, anarchism, and literature; street actions and imprisonment; anarchism and modern humanity; and anarchist theology. There were also roundtables and workshops on anarchist pedagogy, surveillance security, and bodily health and safety during militant actions. I can honestly say I have never attended a conference where, in the same afternoon, I learned about nineteenth-century South American free love, *and then* I learned how to wash chemical deterrents out of eyes during a street action. Nor have I ever been to a conference—or anywhere, really— where a woman felt comfortable enough to breastfeed her child during the middle of her talk without skipping a beat. It was a rupture in time and space that we all needed.

I went into organizing this conference with the knowledge that very few contemporary anarchist scholars connect anarchism and the body except through sexuality or sexual experience, often through the domain of gender studies. Although my own research is grounded in gender studies, I wondered what I was missing by

---
* Michelle M. Campbell is a doctoral candidate in nineteenth-century American literature at Purdue University. Her dissertation examines nineteenth-century Midwestern Anarchist women writers, including Lucy Parsons, Voltairine de Cleyre, Lizzie Swank Holmes, and Lois Waisbrooker. Her scholarship can be found in *Anarchist Developments in Cultural Studies, MidAmerica*, and the introduction to Lizzie Swank Holme's recovered 1893 anarchist-feminist novel *Hagar Lyndon: Or, A Woman's Rebellion*, which is forthcoming in 2018 from Hastings College Press.

viewing the body only through that particular lens, especially as an anarchist scholar. Do contemporary anarchist scholars examine the possibilities of our minds? Yes. The ethics of our souls? Certainly. I wondered: what weren't we saying about the bodies we lived in and through? How do anarchist activists, theorists, and educators think, act, and exist bodily with themselves and with others? The original call for papers illustrates some of these concerns: "This conference seeks to be the first of its kind that is dedicated to questions of anarchism in conjunction with questions about the body conceived of as real, social, perceived, constructed, or institutionalized. [. . .] We encourage innovative papers that engage with multiple aspects of anarchism intersecting with multiple disciplines and fields."

We were certainly not the first to wonder or write on these questions. Classical anarchist feminists like Voltairine de Cleyre and Emma Goldman linked the female body to patriarchal and state domination through labor and marriage in the late nineteenth and early twentieth centuries. In her essay "Sex Slavery," de Cleyre writes, "Let Woman ask herself, "Why am I the slave of Man? Why is my brain said not to be the equal of his brain? Why is my work not paid equally with his? Why must my body be controlled by my husband?" (2016: 348-9). Indeed, for de Cleyre, the domination of the mind and the body are of equal importance: "These two things, the mind domination of the Church, and the body domination of the State are the causes of sex slavery" (2016: 352). Likewise, Emma Goldman links marriage and capitalism in her essay, "Marriage and Love" because they are both institutions that poison the body (1910: 241). Similarly, in her definitive essay "Anarchism: What It Stands For," Goldman explains, "Real wealth consists in things of utility and beauty, in things that help to create strong, beautiful bodies and surroundings inspiring to live in" (1910: 61). For both de Cleyre and Goldman, consideration of the physical body was not only foundational to their anarchist critiques of domination, but it was also integral to their visions of successful liberation.

Over one hundred years since the time of de Cleyre and Goldman, most contemporary anarchist theorists today connect anarchism and the body through sexuality. Jamie Heckert (2011), in "Sexuality as a State Form," explores the intersection between queer anarchism and poststructuralist articulations of power and biopolitics. Heckert both critiques and explores the ways in which representation, particularly of the body or its performativity, can enact violence through speaking for an individual rather than allowing the individual to speak for themselves. In her article "Constructing Anarchist Sexuality: Queer Identity, Culture, and Politics in the Anarchist Movement," Laura Portwood-Stacer (2010) uses interviews with contemporary North American Anarchists to explore how queer critiques are used within anarchist circles and communities. Her goal is to invest in an authentic identity that resists dominant sexual norms as a strategy for anarchist political projects. From her ethnographic evidence, Portwood-Stacer concludes that there are several pitfalls in attempting to create a queer anarchonormativity. The author also concludes that sexual identity politics, when performed collectively, are a useful tool for fighting against social norms. However, the power used to enforce such a sexuality within anarchist communities needs to be wielded in a way that "maximize[s] those effect[s] that contribute to emancipatory political projects, and minimize those that do not" (2010: 491).

Anarchism and sexuality can also be about refusing to participate in hegemonic structures of domination or engaging in participatory actions that subvert or undermine those same structures. Breanne Fahs in her article "Radical Refusals: On the Anarchist Politics of Women Choosing Asexuality" (2010) suggests that asexuality has been a lifestyle and political maneuver for sexual and gender equality that has long been forgotten. She reviews the history of the "sexual liberation" of women during second-wave feminism in order to detail the problems of both sexual repression and sexual "freedom" in a system of state and patriarchal control. Fahs argues that sexually liberated women are still participating in a system of repression when engaging in acts with multiple partners and sex without consequences because women are expected to be sexual. This expectation strips women of the agency to decide their own sexual wants and needs. Fahs argues that asexuality may be helpful "to dismantle the entire institution of sex" (2010: 451). By refusing to participate in any sexual activity, Fahs explains, women are able to rob the institution of its power over bodies and relationships. In "Post-Anarchism and the Contrasexual," Lena Eckert (2011) connects the metaphor of the dildo from Beatriz Preciado's *Contrasexual Manifesto* with that of Haraway's cyborg. Eckert explains that the dildo is effective in undermining "hegemonic structures of desire, pleasure and bodies when applied as a subversive quotation. Quoting or mapping the dildo on any body part (or the entirety of the body) means to question the body as a sexual contest; it questions the possibility of framing or defining the context" (2011: 81).

A notable exception to the scholarship linking anarchism and sexuality is Richard Cleminson's "Making Sense of the Body: Anarchism, Nudism and Subjective Experience" (2004). For early twentieth Spanish anarchists in particular, Cleminson argues, "the body [...] and the social relations that emanated from it and around it, came to be a material resource as well as a discursive device on which anarchists bestowed significations that allowed them to denounce capitalist social relations" (2004: 715). For these anarchists, the body and its experiential processes were deeply ingrained in their political becoming. These influential essays began the conversation about what anarchist scholarship can bring to bear on the question of the body. This special edition aims to continue and complicate that conversation.

Two essays included in this special edition, which were original to the "Anarchism and the Body" Conference, expand our understanding of the gendered and the geographical body, moving away from a white North American or Western European understanding of anarchism and the body. Benjamin H. Abbot's "'That Monster Cannot Be a Woman': Queerness and Treason in the Partido Liberal Mexicano" and Mariel M. Acosta Matos's "Graphic Representations of Grammatical Gender in Spanish Language Anarchist Publications" are new voices in the study of anarchism and the body. For Abbot, an important part of recovering anarchist history is to show the ways in which anarchist narratives both reinforced and complicated gender roles in the early nineteenth century Mexico. Ey examines the ways in which this played out in Ricardo Flores Magón's Partido Liberal Mexicano (the Mexican Liberal Party), the first coordinated movement against the Mexican dictator, Porfirio Díaz, especially through the gendered rhetoric used in dissident newspaper *Regeneración*, a publication Magón wrote for while jailed. Along the same lines, Acosta investigates what she has coined as "Graphic Alternatives to Grammatical Gender," or "GAGG" in Spanish language anarchist publications in the last fifty years. Through a linguistic and rhetorical study, Acosta finds numerous graphic representations that both subvert and reject linguistic sexism that has encoded gender norms into orthography. Not only are textual artifacts important for our study of the history of anarchism and the body, but they can also help to shape the possibilities of our future through suggesting possibilities of becoming.

Lewis Call's "'A Thought Thinking Itself': Postanarchism in Grant Morrison's *The Invisibles*" is an important analysis of the ways in which a text can both exemplify and influence postanarchism through subversion, fragmentation, the imaginary, and the symbolic. Call's emphasis on the visual imaginary to resist the symbolic as well as the fragmentation of subjectivity to recuperate the Symbolic serves to illustrate the ways in which literary and graphic representations (or subversions thereof) can create a roadmap for thinking anarchistically about bodies, their performativity, and their elusiveness.

Bodily inquiry doesn't need to stay in the realm of feminism and gender studies; the final two papers are a few steps away from that stricture. Jesse Cohn's translations of "Christopher's" "The Affective Bases of Domination" and Daniel Colson's "Proudhon, Lacan, et les points de capiton" help point us in a different, more theoretical direction. "Christopher" argues for a libertarian pedagogy that incorporates emotional education in order to heal the fragmentation of mind and body. Such a pedagogy, he explains, can serve to help subvert systems of domination while taking into account both psychoanalytic thought and contemporary neurobiological research. This affective treatment would enable individuals to resist hegemonic ideology and affirm the basic tenets of an anarchist or communist community through an "interdependent individuality" grounded in empathy. The second translated work was written by Daniel Colson. It brings the Lacanian concept of *les points de capiton* (quilting points) to bear on Proudhonian interpretations of the individual. In his introduction to the Colson translation, Jesse Cohn aptly describes the result of Colson's essay as revealing a Proudhon who "in fact launches a pluralistic assault on all the utopias that aim to reduce human diversity to a single normative image, an inevitably despotic 'Absolute.'" Colson's argument will hopefully renew interest in Proudhon as an important theorist from whom we still have much to learn.

This special edition of *Anarchist Developments in Cultural Studies* serves, I hope, as a beginning for anarchist and radical scholars to continue to reach beyond or build on an already established body of work. Much work remains to be done not only to work through, postulate, and discover/recover anarchist accounts of the body, but to use methodologies and theories particular to anarchist studies that can help us consider bodily difference, its artefactual representations, and possibilities for future (in)habitation.

Works Cited

Cleminson, Richard. (2004) "Making Sense of the Body: Anarchism, Nudism and Subjective Experience." *Bulletin of Spanish Studies* 81.6: pp. 697-716.

De Cleyre, Voltairine. [1914] (2016) "Sex Slavery." *The Selected Works of Voltairine de Cleyre*. Ed. Alexander Berkman. Oakland: AK Press. pp. 342-358.

Eckert, Lena. (2011) "Post(-)anarchism and the Contrasexual Practices of Cyborgs in Dildotopia Or 'The War on the Phallus.'" *Anarchism and Sexuality: Ethics Relationships and Power*. Eds. Jamie Heckert and Richard Cleminson. New York: Routledge. pp. 69-92.

Fahs, Breanne. (2010) "Radical Refusals: On the Anarchist Politics of Women Choosing Asexuality." *Sexualities* 13.4: pp. 445-461.

Goldman, Emma. (1910) "Marriage and Love." *Anarchism and Other Essays*. New York: Mother Earth Publishing Co. pp. 233-246.

Goldman, Emma. "Anarchism: (1910) What It Really Stands For." *Anarchism and Other Essays*. New York: Mother Earth Publishing Co. pp. 53-74.

Heckert, Jamie. (2011) "Sexuality as a State Form." *Post-Anarchism: A Reader*. Eds. Sureyyya Evren and Duane Rousselle. London: Pluto Press, pp. 195-207.

Portwood-Stacer, Laura. (2010) "Constructing Anarchist Sexuality: Queer Identity, Culture, and Politics in the Anarchist Movement." *Sexualities* 13.4: pp. 479-493.

2.

"That Monster Cannot Be a Woman:"
Queerness and Treason in the Partido Liberal Mexicano

Benjamin H. Abbott*

The year 1901 marked a turning point for Mexican dialogues on gender and sexuality as well as on national politics. At the first Congreso Liberal in San Luis Potosí early in the year, journalist Ricardo Flores Magón fiercely denounced the administration of Porfirio Díaz as a "den of thieves."[1] Díaz cracked down, throwing Ricardo Flores Magón and other troublemakers into the infamous Belén prison in Mexico City. Despite this, Ricardo Flores Magón continued to write for the dissident newspaper *Regeneración* from his cell until Díaz shut the paper down in October. Just one month later, Mexico City police raided a party and arrested forty-one people identified as men half of whom wore elegant dresses. The city incarcerated these dancers in *Belén* "for attacks on morality,"[2] eventually sending nineteen of them off to forced labor in Yucatán as part of the Mexican government's military campaign against Mayan Indians. Both the political transgression of rebels like Ricardo Flores Magón and the gender transgression of "the famous 41" invoked the wrath of the state and attracted considerable public attention. Open discussion on the previously taboo subjects of Díaz opposition and male homosexuality proliferated. Newspapers covered the 41 with a mixture of fascination, celebration, and condemnation; the group became an enduring symbol for the Mexican queer community. Ricardo Flores Magón's "Partido Liberal Mexicano" served as the first coordinated movement against the dictator.[3]

A few years earlier, the consummate anti-radical Dr. James Weir, Jr. expressed the fear that soon some "professional anarchist" would lead an "army of degenerates, composed of anarchists, nihilists, sexual perverts, and congenital criminals, against

* Benjamin H. Abbott is a PhD student, anarchist, and science fiction author. Eir interest in radical politics and the humanities began with reading Howard Zinn's *A People's History of the United States* as a teenager. Learning about the Plan de Sain Diego uprising and working with Ricard Slatta convinced em to pursue an MA in History at the University of New Mexico. In that program, Benjamin developed a focus on the international anarchist movement in the era of Mexican Revolution. Ey joined American Studies on the advice of friends and professors. Eir current research looks at narratives of the body—gender, sexuality, race—across the Partido Liberal Mexicano and its allies. Contact Benjamin at benjamin.abbott@gmail.com

[1] Spanish "una madriguera de bandidos" in Ethel Duffy Turner. (2003) [1984] *Ricardo Flores Magón y el Partido Liberal Mexicano*. Mexico City: Comisión Nacional Editorial del C.E.N., p. 32. All translations are mine unless otherwise noted.

[2] Robert McKee Irwin. (2003) *Mexican Masculinities*. Minneapolis: University of Minnesota Press, pp. 66-9.

[3] Chaz Bufe & Mitchell Cowen Veter, Eds. (2005) *Dreams of Freedom: A Ricardo Flores Magón Reader*. Oakland, California: AK Press, p. 33; "El Baile de los 41: 19 de los Consignados Remitidos a Yucatán," *El Popular*, November 23, 1901.

society."[4] No such alliance between queers and anarchists emerged in Ricardo Flores Magón's Partido Liberal Mexicano (PLM), which became a vibrant part the international anarchist movement in exile in the United States. To the contrary, Ricardo Flores Magón and others PLM members denounced political opponents with masculinist anti-queer slurs and made appeals to natural heterosexuality. PLM rhetoric on gender and sexual transgression often mirrors the eugenicist discourse of degeneracy that Weir's writings exemplify. While Weir worried groups he despised as unfit and atavistic would band together, the anarchist PLM operated within a partially shared conceptual framework that denigrated queerness. Instead of finding commonality in the state and social persecution the 41 and other queers faced, the PLM used queerness in general and the 41 specifically as signs bourgeois degeneracy counter to the party's revolutionary message.[5]

Weir's nightmares are my dreams. His apocalyptic vision of anarchists and sexual perverts waging war on civilization illustrates a possibility unfulfilled in the PLM. I lament the historical and sometimes present lack of solidarity between anti-capitalist radicals and queers, two categories that of course overlapped then and overlap today. My study comes out of this absence, this alliance that could have been but wasn't. I want to take the contradictions and violence of history seriously rather than papering them over in the service a heroic narrative (as much as I enjoy anarchist heroic narratives). My analysis speaks to how systems of oppressions are intricately connected, mutually reinforcing, and remarkably malleable. In conversation with Nicole Guidotti-Hernández's *Unspeakable Violence* (2011), I argue for the critical study of historical revolutionary movements as part of the continuing radical project. I echo Guidotti-Hernández's skepticism of heroic resistance narratives but without the desire to discard them entirely.[6] The passionate and uncompromising social-justice rhetoric of Ricardo Flores Magón in particular continues to inspire Mexicans, Chicanos, and leftists of all nationalities even in the present day. A re-examination of gender relations in the form of women's liberation constituted a key element of the party's ideology. Historians have long recognized the PLM for this body of thought and for the participation of women within the party. As Emma Pérez writes, the PLM provided a space for women to articulate their critiques of male supremacy and support the radical cause in their own terms.[7] In an imagined revolutionary future, Omar Ramírez leaves a resurrected Ricardo Flores Magón to receive "the praise and

---

[4] James Weir, Jr.. (1897) *The Psychical Correlation of Religious Emotion and Sexual Desire*. Louisville, KY: Courier-Journal Job Printing Co., p. 337.

[5] I use "queers" to refer to those constructed as gender and/or sexually deviant and abnormal. In addition to decrying anti-capitalism as degenerate, Weir denounced the women's suffrage movement in similar terms.

[6] Nicole M. Guidotti-Hernandez. (2011) *Unspeakable Violence: Remapping US and Mexican National Imaginaries*. Durham: Duke University Press, pp. 3-4.

[7] Emma Pérez. (1999) *The Decolonial Imaginary: Writing Chicanas into History*. Bloomington: University of Indiana Press, pp. 55-6.

criticism he never had the chance to experience after his death so long ago."[8] I strive for the same combination in my treatment of the PLM.

This essay centers on the intersection of these two themes of egalitarian social revolution and gender definition embodied by the simultaneous incarceration of political and sexual deviants. PLM notables such as Ricardo Flores Magón articulated a vision of gender based on the biological binary of men and women, but rife with ambiguities and contradictions. This vision exalted a revolutionary masculinity characterized by productive labor and violent defense of independence, while denigrating effeminacy and homosexuality as its antithesis. Consistent with the grand trend of period revolutionary discourse on the subject, various PLM writers employed the 41 as the epitome of aristocratic degeneracy, indulgence, and treason to the nation and people. These PLM writers rhetorically constructed this form of gender transgression as worthy of scorn and shunning from the mass of allegedly normal working-class men and women. Correct masculine behavior existed in contrast with these cowardly, treacherous deviants. Thus, the elite transvestite homosexual functioned as a key symbol for defining class struggle. The PLM produced the ideal of popular manhood in conjunction with shadow of the queer. This matches common attitudes and persuasive techniques in European circles as well as contrasting with those of other anarchists—particularly Germans and the Russian-American Emma Goldman—who promoted acceptance of homosexuality as a component of social transformation.[9]

I argue that writers within PLM's orbit employed contradictory and contested narratives of gender, drawn from different sources and varying both by author and circumstances. Anarchist theories about individual freedom as well as proletarian women as slaves suffering a double oppression interacted with scientific and traditional notions of natural roles for each gender. Masculine concepts such as fraternity and status competition took on particular revolutionary permutations. Practical experience at times came into conflict with gender tropes. Regardless of what the men in the movement may have wanted, PLM practice showed that sometimes women proved superior warriors and attempts at patriarchal control sometimes failed. The ambiguities and contradictions of the party's sexual narrative stand out in stark relief on the subject of feminine gender transgression. While PLM authors consistently employed the image of effeminate homosexuality derogatively, as described above, their portrayal of gender transgression from women varied from pejorative to celebratory. *Regeneración* articles condemned bourgeois feminists for wanting to become men at the same time they extolled virile revolutionary women; they assigned the martial labor of combat exclusively to men in theory, yet simultaneously praised individual women who excelled as warriors. This matches the best current literature on gender articulation both in Mexico and elsewhere that

---

[8] Omar Ramírez. (2008) "Black Flag, Red Heart: A Study of Chicano and Chicana Anarchy," M.A. Thesis California State University, Northridge, p. 51.

[9] Terence Kissack. (2008) *Free Comrades: Anarchism and Homosexuality in the United States 1895-1917*. Oakland: AK Press; Gert Hekma, Harry Oosterhuis, & James Steakley, Eds. (1995) *Gay Men and the Sexual History of the Political Left*. New York: The Hayworth Press, Inc..

stresses complexity, contingency, and the necessity of transcending simplistic stereotypes. None of this nuance diminishes the intensity and horror of gender inequality or discrimination in either the past or present.[10]

Because my analysis relies heavily on pieces from the PLM periodical *Regeneración*, a brief discussion of that paper and its context is in order. It began in 1900 as a relatively innocuous Mexico City publication on legal procedure. Ricardo Flores Magón's more academically and financially successful brother Jesús served as one of the original editors. The paper started to attack the government more openly as the Liberal movement grew and particularly as Ricardo Flores Magón's influence on it increased. This prompted the repression mentioned above, which terminated the periodical at the end of 1901. Regeneración reappeared in San Antonio, Texas in 1904 after various PLM members came to the United States to escape death or imprisonment at the hands of Díaz. From this point on, Ricardo Flores Magón's importance to the paper as well as the influence of anarchism steadily grew. During this period, the PLM shifted from a mixed coalition united under the wide banner of liberal reform to an unabashedly anarchist group advocating the complete abolition of economic, political, and spiritual hierarchy.

At its height, *Regeneración* could boast of tens of thousands of subscribers. By the time the paper moved to Los Angeles, California, subscribers constituted a diverse group: local railroad workers and other laborers, Mexican exiles from various classes, and ideological allies of countless nationalities and economic backgrounds. Francisco Madero's rise to preeminence in the anti-Díaz movement in 1910 marked a pivotal time for both the party and *Regeneración*. Many former PLM supporters turned to Madero, despite Ricardo Flores Magón's insistence that he was a bourgeois oppressor who would resist rather than enact revolutionary social transformation. These defections to Madero increased as opponents persuasively, though inaccurately, presented the PLM's campaign in Baja California as treasonous filibustering. Ricardo Flores Magón considered each defection a personal betrayal and the traditional PLM core dwindled. At the same time, however, a vibrant PLM and larger radical community existed in Los Angeles. Associated periodicals such as the Colombian anarchist Blanca de Moncaleano's *Pluma roja* published alongside *Regeneración*. This paralleled the earlier explosion of PLM-related papers along the Texas border. These are the spaces that Pérez identifies as enabling PLM women to articulate their own voices and positions.[11]

---

[10] Héctor Domínguez-Ruvalcaba. (2007) *Modernity and the Nation in Mexican representations of Masculinity: From Sensuality to Bloodshed*. New York: Palgrave Macmillan, pp. 1-7; Irwin, Edward J. McCaughan, & Michelle Rocío Nasser (2003) "Introduction" in *The Famous 41: Sexuality and Social Control in Mexico, c. 1901*. New York: Palgrave Macmillan, p. 12; Robert McKee Irwin. (2003) *Mexican Masculinities*. Minneapolis: University of Minnesota Press, pp. 66-9.

[11] Ethel Duffy Turner. (2003) [1984] *Ricardo Flores Magón y el Partido Liberal Mexicano*. Mexico City: Comisión Nacional Editorial del C.E.N., pp. 22-61; William D. Estrada. (2008) *The Los Angeles Plaza: Sacred and Contested Spaces*. Austin: University of Texas Press, pp. 143-4; Juan Gómez-Quiñones. (1973) *Sembradores, Ricardo Flores Magon y el Partido Liberal Mexicano: A Eulogy and Critique*. Los Angeles: Aztlán Publications, pp. 23-52; James A. Sandos. (1992) *Rebellion in the Borderlands*. Norman: University of Oklahoma Press, p. 130.

This project responds to historian Joan Wallach Scott famous call for history that engages gender as a meaningful category of analysis. *The Decolonial Imaginary* (1999) by Emma Pérez and the article "Transborder Discourse" (2003) by Clara Lomas serve as my chief inspirations as well the closest scholarship both in subject matter and theoretical approach. In the aforementioned book, Pérez employs Foucault's discursive method that takes nothing for granted and encourages questioning assumptions. Foucault, by Pérez's description, treated everything as a product of language, thus making meaning a matter of continual renegotiation. In particular, Pérez draws on Scott's interpretation and use of Foucault crafted specifically for the purpose of exploring how and why gender has been linguistically constructed and utilized in various periods. Pérez answers Scott's request for historiography that looks deeply and critically at gender. She wields this method in order to recover lost Chicana stories, which she defines broadly, that were previously hidden or neglected.[12]

Pérez identifies the PLM as one of the few examples of revolutionary fervor and intellectual opening that enabled Chicana feminist voices to emerge during the period. In this section of the book she explicates how Ricardo and the other male PLM members argued for women's liberation while simultaneously maintaining patriarchal notions about a woman's place in the struggle and her essential characteristics. For instance, the 1910 *Regeneración* address to women exhorted them to demand that the men in their lives take up the gun against Díaz rather than do so themselves. Beyond the analysis of PLM rhetoric, Pérez conducted an interview with a PLM supporter who noted the gendered division of labor at the party's communal farm in the Silver Lake area of Los Angeles. She attributes these apparent contradictions to the "historical moment" that "ascribed to a particular politics and knowledge about women, their rights and inherent biological traits."[13] Pérez demonstrates how women within the PLM scene, most notably Moncaleano with her lucid criticism against sexism from revolutionary men, furthered the radical cause while challenging, both subtly and explicitly, the dominant gender ideology of tacit male supremacy.

In her article, Lomas expands upon this research by focusing specifically on the rhetoric about gender used by female writers such as Moncaleano in leftist periodicals in the borderlands. Like Pérez, she explicates the ways by which politically active women rejected androcentric narratives of revolution and developed their own instead. More than Pérez, Lomas zeroes in on Moncaleano and the periodical *Pluma roja* as the strongest dissident voice against patriarchal practices within the PLM. These two works form a firm practical and theoretical foundation for this project.[14]

---

[12] Pérez, pp. xiii-xvii.

[13] Ibid., p. 57.

[14] Clara Lomas, "Transborder Discourse: The Articulation of Gender in the Borderlands in the Early Twentieth Century," *Frontiers: A Journal of Women Studies*, Vol. 24, Nos. 2 & 3 (2003): pp. 51-74.

As the bulk of the research on gender and the PLM has dealt with conceptions of women and femininity, I have a particular interest in also critically investigating representations of men and masculinity. While pioneering scholars have explicated the PLM's contradictory ideology on women, which embraced liberation and equality alongside the acceptance of natural female roles, the way the PLM's understanding on masculinity interacted with these views has gone largely unexplored. I seek a fuller understanding of the "masculinist revolutionary rhetoric" that Pérez identifies as the party default.[15]

Pérez briefly refers to gender ideology of European radicals like Mikhail Bakunin and Peter Kropotkin as influential within the PLM. The collection *Gay Men and the Sexual History of the Political Left* provides fuller international context for anarchist and socialist perspectives on sexuality before, during, and after the period. The revolutionary left at the time had deep connections across the world; even relatively obscure publications such as Moncaleano's *Pluma roja* might find their way into the hands of anarchist readers in Spain. The book's introductory overview highlights the prevalence of then-scientific gender essentialism among leftists and the common construction of homosexuality as an aristocratic or bourgeois vice contrasted with the masculine purity of the working class. Hubert Kennedy's piece "Johann Baptist von Schweitzer: The Queer Marx Loved to Hate" shows how Karl Marx and Friedrich Engels disdained homosexuality as an unnatural elite corruption in their personal communications. "Male Inverts and Homosexuals" by Richard Cleminson shows similar dynamics at play within the Spanish anarchist periodical *Revista Blanca* between 1898 and the 1930s. On the other hand, Saskia Poldervaart's essay demonstrates the nuanced views on sexuality of early utopian socialists and "Anarchism and Homosexuality in Wilhelmine Germany" by Walter Fähnders details pro-queer advocacy by German anarchists around the turn of the century. The book shows the left in era of the PLM held conflicts about gender and sexuality alongside the master narrative of heterosexuality as natural and correct.[16]

While the study of gender and labor in Latin America as a whole has massive body of scholarship, works that apply directly to Mexico in the era of the Mexican Revolution are relatively scarce. The literature on anarchism and gender across Latin America supports the above picture of revolutionary groups opening space for feminist critiques while simultaneously retaining the ideology of masculine supremacy. In *Imposing Decency* (1999), Eileen J. Suárez Findlay shows the limits of the Puerto Rican male left's interest in challenging sexual norms. Her exploration of anarchist-feminist Luisa Capetillo's thought reveals how much it resembles Moncaleano's and in this way connects with Lomas's work. Maxine Molyneux's article "No God, No Boss, No Husband" (1986) provides similar resonances through a discussion of the short-lived Argentine anarchist-feminist publication La *Voz de la Muje*. Molyneux notes the lack of solidarity from anarchist men in *La Voz's* feminist struggle as well as how Argentine anarchist-feminist continued to impose appropriate sexuality on the traditional heterosexual reproductive model. Finally,

---

[15] Pérez, p. 57.

[16] Hekma et al., pp. 7-8, 41, 71, 117, 259.

Elizabeth Quay Hutchison's article "From 'Mujer Esclava' to 'Mujer Limón'" demonstrates how the Chilean anarchist discourse on women in the early part of the twentieth century existed within a patriarchal framework. This scholarship suggests a masculine-supremacist dynamic of constrained women's emancipation that stretched across the Spanish-language anarchist community around the turn of the twentieth century.[17]

On Mexican masculinity specifically, the ethnography and theoretical contribution of Matthew C. Gutmann and Robert McKee Irwin's historically minded literary analysis is most relevant. Gutmann wrote the path-breaking 1996 field study of men as men in Colonia Santo Domingo in Mexico. Gutmann emphasizes the "ambiguity, confusion, and contradiction in male identities."[18] He criticizes scholars for blithely accepting the rigid stereotype of the Mexican macho and a unitary, universal Mexican masculinity. While we must exercise caution in using the 1990s to say anything about the 1900s and 1910s, his concept of the "contradictory consciousness" produced by the tension of "consciousness inherited uncritically from the past and consciousness developed in the course of practically transforming the world" perhaps has its parallels for the PLM.[19] Gutmann also offers a long and thoughtful introduction to the collection *Changing Men and Masculinities in Latin America* that makes many of the same points as well as underlines the acknowledgment of gender inequality as foundational to studying masculinity in Latin America.[20]

Irwin provides a kindred theoretical framework in *Mexican Masculinities* (2003). Drawing on both period sources and cutting-edge gender scholarship, he introduces the concept of gender as a continuum that ranges from very masculine to very feminine and shows the notion of masculinity as performance has a long history in the literature. Echoing Gutmann but going further, he describes Mexican masculinity as a "messy web of contradictions."[21] Irwin details a complex historical progression centering on 1901 and the famous 41, when Mexican discourse on gender and sexuality began to shift from earlier often erotic upper-class narratives of homosocial bonding to the exaltation of lower-class masculinity that had before been characterized as barbaric. Irwin's scholarship provides understanding of the context and intricacies behind PLM expressions of masculinity.

---

[17] Eileen J. Suárez Findlay. (1999) *Imposing Decency: The Politics of Sexuality and Race in Puerto Rico, 1870-1920*. Durham: Duke University Press, pp. 135-66; Maxine Molyneux. (1986) "No God, No Boss, No Husband: Anarchist Feminism in Nineteenth-Century Argentina," *Latin American Perspectives* Vol. 13 No. 1 (Winter), pp. 119-145; Elizabeth Quay Hutchison. (2001) *'From 'La Mujer Esclava' to 'La Mujer Limón:' Anarchism and the Politics of Sexuality in Early-Twentieth-Century Chile,"* Hispanic American Historical Review, *Vol. 81 No. 3-4 (August-November), pp. 519-553.*

[18] Matthew C. Gutmann. (2007) *The Meanings of Macho: Being a Man in Mexico City*. Berkeley: University of California Press, p. 243.

[19] Ibid., p. 243.

[20] Matthew C. Gutmann. (2003) *Changing Men and Masculinities in Latin America*. Duke University Press. pp. 1-2.

[21] Robert McKee Irwin. (2003) *Mexican Masculinities*. Minneapolis: University of Minnesota Press, pp. xix-xxii.

With regards to the rest of the scholarship on gender related to the Mexican Revolution, the collection *Sex in Revolution* (2006) stands out. In the forward, Carlos Monsiváis writes in support of the Pérez thesis of the PLM as a locus of gender radicalism within the period. Gabriela Cano's chapter entitled "Unconcealable Realities of Desire: Amelio Robles's (Transgender) Masculinity in the Mexican Revolution" (2006) provides both a compelling story and rich detail on conceptions of gender during the period. Her insights on the aggressive character of revolutionary masculinity, the acceptance of masculinized females coupled with disdain for effeminate males, and the conflation of masculinity with national identity resonate with the earlier work such as Irwin as well as my own research here. In *Compromised Positions* (2001), another outstanding recent book, Katherine Elaine Bliss analyzes prostitution in Mexico City from the Porfiriato into the 1940s. In particular relevance with this project, she studies masculinity as it related to prostitution and ultimately blames the acceptance of the dominant masculinist ideology as critical in explaining the failure of government campaigns to end the practice. Acceptance of and inability to confront masculine sexual entitlement and privilege prevented these campaigns from being successful. Taking *Compromised Positions* together with *Sex in Revolution*, recent gender research on the Mexican Revolution stresses its failure to fulfill the promise of women's emancipation as well as the value of seriously investigating gender ideologies that lead to this predicament.[22]

Widely recognized as influential precursors to the Mexican Revolution, Ricardo Flores Magón and the PLM in general have generated a considerable body of work in both Spanish and English. Though the famous historian and Chicano activist Juan Gómez-Quiñones notes the "role of women"[23] within the PLM as one of the three "historically interesting"[24] things about the party, the scholarship devotes the lion's share of the attention to the men without any investigation of their construction of masculinity. Gómez-Quiñones himself does not depart from this model. It reflects the greater power and prominence of the male PLM leadership at the time as well as the interests of academia. Historically, gender analysis is a relatively recent phenomenon. I maintain that gender ideologies and conceptions of masculinity and femininity are critically important in understanding both the course of PLM history as well as that of the Mexican Revolution as a whole. Gender plays a fundamental part in human social organization; the PLM heavily employed gendered appeals to incite revolutionary action.

Past his key position in the disputed precursor movement, Ricardo Flores Magón personally tends to be treated as either a heroic liberator or an earnest but unrealistic dreamer. The work of Ethel Duffy Turner, a one-time supporter and close associate, typifies the former view. She portrayed him as a driven and unbending visionary

---

[22] Jocelyn Olcott, Mary K. Vaughan, & Gabriela Cano, Eds. (2006) *Sex in Revolution: Gender, Politics and Power in Modern Mexico*. Duke University Press, pp. 2-4.

[23] Juan Gómez-Quiñones. (1973) *Sembradores, Ricardo Flores Magon y el Partido Liberal Mexicano: A Eulogy and Critique*. Los Angeles: Aztlán Publications, p. 30.

[24] Ibid., p. 31.

almost beyond reproach, a sort of revolutionary saint or prophet. At the same time, she emphasized his communistic goal of universally extending the good life, she downplayed his anarchist opposition to all governments. This aligns with her political persuasion as a socialist more accepting of the state; she left a job as English-language editor of *Regeneración* in the climate of American socialist criticism of the PLM's increasingly open anarchist views. Consistent with Pérez's description of Turner as uninterested in analyzing gender while on the PLM staff, she gave little space to either the party's ideas on the subject or the women involved with the PLM. Authors such as Colin M. MacLachlan and Ward S. Albro, on the other hand, stress the impracticality of Magón's anarchism rather than the party's aims and operations.[25]

This absence of gender conforms to the two major syntheses of the Mexican Revolution, by John Mason Hart and Alan Knight respectively. Women and gender analysis play next to no role. Hart neglects textual sources on female revolutionaries and simply provides photographs. Knight suggests scholars look to elite women materially involved in the fighting rather than marginal female intellectuals. This matches his overall dismissal of ideology in the Mexican Revolution. He rejects the traditional conceptualization of the PLM as a meaningful precursor to Madero's rise. Instead, they only attracted initial support because of their early monopoly on opposition politics. Hart likewise throws out the notion of distinct precursor movement, but for antithetical reasons. He sees the PLM as setting off the Mexican Revolution proper even before Madero. All of this demonstrates the novelty of Pérez's scholarship. It is telling how she engages with the work of Gómez-Quiñones; he at least made mention of the importance of women within the PLM. Much subsequent scholarship did not.

As a gateway into exploring these constructions, I begin with the mainstream PLM position on gender that comes out most clearly in two articles from 1910 published respectively by Ricardo Flores Magón and Práxedis Guerrero, a prominent theorist and combatant in the field who became revered as martyr after he died in action at the end of the year. The Guerrero piece goes into greater detail about the thought underlying PLM views. The notion of a natural order between the sexes in which each has proper roles emerges as central in this text, a theme that permeates the PLM's and broader anarchist discourse. Like Magón, Guerrero reviewed the history of the oppression of women across cultures and presented the demand for the equality of men and women as an essential revolutionary position. In the forward to *Sex in Revolution*, Monsiváis quotes Guerrero as a simple—and rare—supporter of women's liberation in the period. We should remember that Guerrero went on to dismiss feminism as a gender-bending bourgeois distraction: "Not being able to be a woman[,] the woman wants to be a man; she throws herself with the dignified enthusiasm of a more rational feminism in pursuit of all the ugly things men can be

---

[25] Turner (2003) [1984] *Ricardo Flores Magón y el Partido Liberal Mexicano.* Mexico City: Comisión Nacional Editorial del C.E.N.; Ethel Duffy Turner. (1981) *Revolution in Baja California: Ricardo Flores Magón's High Noon.* Detroit: Blaine Ethridge Books; Colin M. MacLachlan. (1991) *Anarchism and the Mexican Revolution: The Political Trials of Ricardo Flores Magón in the United States.* Berkeley: University of California Press, pp. 5, 22, 31-2, 39, 42, 52, 54, 62, 72, 85, 90-1, 111, 118-9; Ward S. Albro (1992) *Always a Rebel: Ricardo Flores Magón and the Mexican Revolution.* Fort Worth: Texas Christian University Press, pp. 30, 133, 137.

and do: she wants to carry out the functions of the police, of lawyers, of the tyrannical politician and to elect along with men the masters of the human race."[26]

While the critique of liberal feminism as reactionary reformism opposed to authentic social revolution was shared by PLM ally Emma Goldman and other radicals, Guerrero's allegation of gender deviancy and masculinization employed in the effort to discredit feminists speak volumes about his conceptions of the subject. He emphasized the point by continuing as follows: "'Feminism' serves as a base of opposition for the enemies of the emancipation of women. Certainly there's nothing attractive in a policewoman, in a woman far from the sweet mission of her sex in order to brandish the whip of oppression, in a woman avoiding her graceful feminine individuality in order to wear the hybridity of 'masculinization.'"[27]

To reinforce the undesirability of upsetting gender norms, Guerrero presented male homosexuality and effeminacy as the prime example of the degeneracy of the upper class. As a counter to claims of the moral fragility of women, Guerrero invoked this narrative of homosexuality. He condemned it as "that infamous prostitution of men, so extended in all countries of the world and practiced scandalously by representatives of the so-called educated classes, between the men of the State and the refined nobility, as the irreverent pen of Maximilian Harden has made it known in Germany, as was discovered in Mexico in an intimate dance of aristocrats."[28] In this fashion, non-conformist gender expressions—whether they involve feminists who want to be men or men who wear dresses and have sex with other men— become a symbol of bourgeois decadency and the antithesis of the revolutionary enterprise. The example of the 41 serves to shame men as a whole.[29]

As a conclusion, Guerrero reiterated that he wanted women's emancipation to come without disrupting 'natural' gender roles and identity. "Libertarian equality," he wrote, "does not try to make men out of women; it gives the same opportunities to the two fractions of the human species in order that both are developed without obstacles, mutually supporting each other, without disturbing the place that each one

---

[26] "No pudiendo ser mujer la mujer quiere ser hombre; se lanza con un entusiasmo digno de un feminismo más racional en pos de todas las cosas feas que un hombre puede ser y hacer: quiere desempeñar funciones de policía, de pica-pleitos, de tirano político y elegir con los hombres los amos del género humano." Práxedis Guerrero. (1910) "La Mujer." *Regeneración*, November 12, 1910, p. 2.

[27] "El 'feminismo' sirve de base á la oposición de los enemigos de la emancipación de la mujer. Ciertamente no hay nada atractivo en una mujer gendarme, en una mujer alejada de la dulce misión de su sexo para empuñar el látigo de la opresión, en una mujer huyendo de su graciosa individualidad femenina para vestir la hibridez del 'honbrunamiento.'" Práxedis Guerrero. (1910) "La Mujer." *Regeneración*, November 12, 1910, p. 2.

[28] "Esa prostitución infame de los hombres, tan extendida en todos los países del mundo y practicada escandalosamente por representantes de las clases llamadas cultas, entre los hombres de Estado y la refinada nobleza, como lo hizo saber la pluma irreverente de Maximiliano Harden, en Alemania, como se descubrió ruidosamente en México en un baile íntimo de aristócratas." Práxedis Guerrero. (1910) "La Mujer." *Regeneración*, November 12, 1910, p. 2.

[29] Héctor Domínguez-Ruvalcaba. (2007) *Modernity and the Nation in Mexican representations of Masculinity: from Sensuality to Bloodshed*. New York: Palgrave Macmillan, pp. 3-4.

has in nature."[30] The alternative he described was perpetual tyranny, slavery, and unhappiness.

Regeneración's earlier attack on former ally Juana Belén Gutiérrez de Mendoza in terms of gender and sexuality after she left the party echoes Guerrero's views about the importance of allegedly natural gender roles in PLM thought. A prominent critic of Díaz, Gutiérrez de Mendoza suffered imprisonment along with Ricardo Flores Magón and his brother Enrique and fled with them across the border into the United States in 1904. Roughly a year later she returned to Mexico and subsequently critiqued PLM operations in Texas. The party core responded in 1906 with a lengthy piece refuting her charges in detail and countering with their own. They began the article with extensive posturing as long-suffering gallants reluctant to fight back against a feminine aggressor out of chivalrous compunctions, who were finally forced to defend their honor. Following a classic technique used when breaking alliances, they claimed Gutiérrez de Mendoza had not rejected them; they had rejected because of "political mercantilism" (*mercantilismo político*) and "disgusting vices" (*repugnantes vicios*).[31] After elaborating on their financial and organizational grievances, the authors condemned Gutiérrez de Mendoza on the basis of sexual morality after a warning to the reader. The slow pace and palpable melodrama in the article continues with a description of how the authors balked when comrades first alerted them of a physical relationship between Gutiérrez de Mendoza and her close friend Elisa Acuña y Rosete:

> We could not conceive that the aforementioned ladies were capable of betraying nature by mutually turning to monstrous and hedonistic delights. We could not believe that Doña Juana B. Gutiérrez de Mendoza, who preaches morality, who styles herself redeemer of peoples, who makes a display of working for the good of the human species, who wants to redeem the Mexican woman, quarrels with nature that so wisely has created the two sexes, in order to turn with her companion Elisa to the sterile and stupid pleasures of Sappho.[32]

---

[30] "La igualdad libertaria no trata de hacer hombre á la mujer; da las mismas oportunidades á las dos fracciones de la especie humana para que ambas se desarrollen sin obstáculos, sirviéndose mutuamente de apoyo, sin estorbarse en el lugar que cada uno tiene en la naturaleza." Práxedis Guerrero. (1910) "La Mujer." *Regeneración,* November 12, 1910, p. 2.

[31] PLM Junta. (1906) "Juana B. Gutiérrez de Mendoza." *Regeneración,* June 15, 1906, pp. 3.

[32] "No podíamos concebir que las mencionadas señoras fueran capaces de traicionar á la naturaleza entregándose mutuamente á deleites monstruosos y hediondos. No podíamos creer que Doña Juana B. Gutiérrez de Mendoza, la que predica moralidad, la que se dice á sí misma redentora de pueblos, la que hace alarde de trabajar por el bien de la especie humana, la que quiere redimir á la mujer mexicana, riñera con la naturaleza que tan sabiamente ha creado los dos sexos, para entregarse con su compañera Elisa á los estériles y estúpidos placeres de Safo." PLM Junta. (1906) "Juana B. Gutiérrez de Mendoza." *Regeneración,* June 15, 1906, pp. 3-4.

The piece holds this note for some paragraphs, providing a salacious account of how the authors saw proof with their "own eyes" (*PROPIOS OJOS*)[33] of the alleged misbehavior and how an in-law of Gutiérrez de Mendoza's who briefly lived in her house had to abruptly flee after he stumbled upon her and Acuña y Rosete engaged in their "favorite pastimes" (*pasatiempos favoritos*).[34] In order to reinforce the narrative of heterosexuality as natural and queerness as a threat, the authors charged the two women with not loving or respecting their parents and excoriated Gutiérrez de Mendoza for dishonoring her excessively tolerant husband. Homosexuality then implies the destruction of the familial order at the heart of society. Like Marx and Engels, the PLM Junta envisioned a post-revolutionary world where queerness would disappear and the supposed natural arrangement of child-rearing man-woman pairs would reign forever. The article concludes with a vicious denunciation of Gutiérrez de Mendoza that unambiguously expels her from the cause if not from the species: "[w]e have sketched the entire body of that hairy being that has lost her sex, who has profaned it and to whom it disgusts us to give the name woman, sacred name that we men all adore, because that monster cannot be a woman, that seedbed of evils, of treacheries, of calumnies, of the blackest betrayals, of ingratitude and meanness, must not have been produced by a human womb."[35]

Though presented more in terms of nature and science than class, this analysis mirrors Guerrero's perspective. Gutiérrez de Mendoza's alleged lesbianism formed a central component of her treacherous character; betraying nature in this fashion matched her political and economic opportunism and duplicity. Within this framework, political and sexual propriety had an inherent connection. Deviation in either area implied deviation in the other. Pietro Gori in a posthumous 1912 *Regeneración* article, belief in the naturalness of reproductive heterosexual coupling established the revolutionary gender order. Gori articulated a vision of a world free from any legal restrictions and moral compunctions that hindered family-oriented and organically evolving man-woman pairings. Queerness constituted rejection of the dreamed-for heterosexual utopia and thus immediately suggested bourgeois subversion, simple criminality, or a combination of the two.[36]

Ricardo Flores Magón's pen-and-ink warfare with former comrade Antonio I. Villareal after the latter left the PLM and began publishing a rival paper entitled

---

[33] Ibid., p. 4.

[34] Ibid.

[35] "Hemos pintado de cuerpo entero á ese hirsuto sér que ha perdido su sexo, que lo ha profanado y á la que nos repugna dar el nombre de mujer, nombre sagrado que todos los hombres adoramos, porque ese monstruo no puede ser mujer, ese almácigo de maldades, de perfidias, de calumnias, de traiciones las más negras, de ingratitudes y de mezquindades, no debe haber sido producido por vientre humano." Ibid.

[36] Susie S. Porter. (2003) "Juana Belén Gutiérrez de Mendoza: Woman of Words, Woman of Actions" in *The Human Tradition in Mexico* (Jeffery M. Pilcher, Ed.) Wilmington, Delaware: SR Books, pp. 103-117; *Regeneración*, June 8, 1912. After briefly supporting Madero, Gutiérrez de Mendoza traveled to Morelos and became a Zapatista colonel. For a further discussion of anarchist narratives of gender that gender on ideas about nature, see Elizabeth Quay Hutchison. (2001) *"From 'La Mujer Esclava' to 'La Mujer Limón:' Anarchism and the Politics of Sexuality in Early-Twentieth-Century Chile,"* Hispanic American Historical Review, Vol. 81 No. 3-4 (August-November), pp. 519-553.

Regeneración corroborates the suspicion that gender transgression in the form of homosexuality (and this time specifically the effeminacy of the 41) operated as a potent symbol and rhetorical tool for members of the party. Magón described various members of the opposing *Regeneración* as well as other foes as "castrates" (*castrados*)[37] and "eunuchs" (*eunucos*),[38] but he fixated on Villarreal's alleged gender deviation at great length. He repeatedly wrote that Villarreal had a homosexual relationship with a barber in Lampazos. In a parallel with the attack on Gutiérrez de Mendoza the Junta made five years prior when Villarreal himself was a respected member and editor of the paper, Ricardo Flores Magón presented this as a damning indictment that he would progressively elaborate on if Villarreal did not relent in his treachery to the proletariat. Earlier, he concluded with the following threat: "[f]or lack of space, I don't talk today about that effeminate barber patron of Antonio I. Villarreal in Lampazos, State of Nuevo León, and, really, not as much for lack of space as for the filthiness of the matter; but if Villarreal wants it, I will publish all that and much more, fitting to appear in the dirty history of the famous Marquis de Sade."[39]

Illustratively, he put this charge of specific same-sex romance alongside that of murder. He apparently thought that this allegation would resonate with his audience because of a shared loathing of male homosexuality. A few issues later Ricardo excoriated Villarreal in an article called "El Coronel de Los 41" in which he described Villarreal as a "pederast" (*pederasta*) and a "queer" (*maricón*).[40] He reiterated the threat of having proof of Villarreal's affair with the effeminate barber. The very next week Ricardo followed up with a piece entitled "Que Hable el Maricón" (Let the Queer Speak) that asked why Villarreal had not responded to the "specific charges" (*cargos concretos*) he had made. Magón rhetorically asked, "[a]re love affairs between one macho and another macho not something shameful?"[41] He went on to equate Villarreal's alleged pederasty with a negation of his status as a man. The brief article finishes on this dramatic note: "Villarreal does not have the right to face any man. He should be spat upon by all men and by all women."[42] In an echo of the Guerrero approach to feminism and PLM condemnation of Gutiérrez de Mendoza, Ricardo Flores Magón here assumed a unity between gender conformers against deviancy.

---

[37] Ricardo Flores Magón (1911). "Degeneración." *Regeneración*, August 12, 1911, p. 1.

[38] Ricardo Flores Magón (1911). "Notas Al Vuelo." *Regeneración*, November 18, 1911, p. 2.

[39] "Por falta de espacio, no hablo hoy de aquel barbero afeminado protector de Antonio I. Villarreal en Lampazos, Estado de Nuevo León, y, realmente, no tanto por la falta de espacio, cuanto por lo sucio del asunto; pero si Villarreal lo quiere, publicaré todo eso y mucho más, digno de figurar en la historia de cieno del famoso Marqués de Sade." Ricardo Flores Magón (1911). "Degeneración," p. 1.

[40] Ricardo Flores Magón. (1911) "El Coronel de Los 41." *Regeneración*, September 16, 1911, p. 2.

[41] "¿No es algo de averguenza el amorío de un macho con un otro macho?" Ricardo Flores Magón. (1911) "Que Hable el Maricón." *Regeneración*, September 23, 1911, p. 3.

[42] "Villarreal no tiene derecho á ver á ningún hombre de frente; Villarreal debe ser escupido por todos los hombres y por todas las mujeres." Ricardo Flores Magón. (1911) "Que Hable el Maricón." *Regeneración*, September 23, 1911, p. 3.

For both Ricardo Flores Magón and Guerrero, gender transgression was fundamentally entangled with notions of honor and of class as well as naturalness. Guerrero presented masculinization as the characteristic of bourgeois feminists while Ricardo Flores Magón emphasized the queerness of Villarreal, whom he identified as a key traitor who abandoned the cause of the working class in order to gain favor with the capitalist bosses. Thus, both presented gender transgression as an example of the perversity of the ruling class and implicitly constructed proletarian gender norms in opposition to this bourgeois degeneracy. A letter from *Regeneración* readers in the same issue discussed above castigated Villarreal specifically for his betrayal of the PLM and followed this with a string of gendered slurs. They wrote, "[t]hat is the shame that you have, effeminate one, sodomite; because of that you have become number 42 of the group of 41."[43] For these PLM supporters, treachery and duplicity went hand in hand with queerness and all three aspects characterized the capitalist in contrast with the workers. The disdain for bourgeois, effeminate, and unnatural homosexuals expressed by Ricardo, Guerrero, and other party members mirrors similar narratives encountered across leftist history.[44]

Conceptions of the honor the transvestite violates form the foundation for PLM articulations of revolutionary masculinity. The exaltation of aggression and bravery—an obviously useful traditional aspect of masculinity to foster when waging a war—served to construct passivity as an affront to all true men. A 1904 *Regeneración* article about a new political slogan that discouraged agitation states: "[t]he eunuchs, the fainthearted, those who in order to insult the virile sex take masculine names, brandish as evidence of impunity the damned phrase with enthusiasm equivalent to their cowardice."[45] This underlines Irwin's description of gender existing on a continuum in men had to perform properly or lose their masculine status.

Within PLM ideology, hard physical labor and exploitation by the bosses characterized the life the working-class man—the kind of man PLM intellectuals wrote about. His identity was wound up within this status as a primary producer of wealth unjustly deprived of the fruits of his labor. According to PLM discourse, this condition of subjugation and servitude inhibited masculinity; a proper man should not accept anyone above him. Picking up the gun and rebelling against all masters typify the PLM manly ideal; countless PLM appeals demand this course. To an extent this channels the notion of aggressive masculinity, that masculinity focuses on endless competition and jockeying for status between men. Octavio Paz popularized a version of this idea based on the verb *chingar*. However, within PLM revolutionary thought the notion of universal brotherhood and radical egalitarianism temper these

---

[43] "Esta es la verguenza que tú gastas, afeminado, sodomo; por eso has ido á ser el 42 del grupo de los 41." Roberto Rodríguez. (1911) "Para Ejemplo." *Regeneración*, September 23, 1911, p. 3.

[44] "Esta es la verguenza que tú gastas, afeminado, sodomo; por eso has ido á ser el 42 del grupo de los 41." *Regeneración*, September 23, 1911; Hekma et al., pp. 7-8, 41, 71, 117, 259.

[45] "Los eunucos, los pusilánimes, los que para afrenta del sexo viril llevan nombres masculinos, enarbolaron como patente de impunidad la frase maldita con entusiasmo equivalente á su cobardía." Ricardo Flores Magón. (1904) La abstención política es la abyección: La política sana y el servilismo." *Regeneración*, December 3, 1904, p. 1.

competitive, combative aspects of masculinity. Ricardo Flores Magón and others advocated not only shooting bosses but working in absolute harmony with comrades and peers. In this way peace, equality, and cooperation formed the natural state with hierarchy existing as the aberration.[46]

The idea of violent resistance as the only acceptable masculine response to domination becomes clear through examination of the gendered character of revolutionary labor described in the PLM press. The PLM called for everyone from elders to children to become involved in the struggle but consistently reserved the role of combatants for men. A 1907 unattributed piece in *Revolución* (a *Regeneración* analogue published in Los Angeles during 1907-1908) entitled "El Deber de la Mujer" (Woman's Duty) included the following passage: "[i]t's necessary, then, to fight against despotism, and each person has to fight according to their sex and age: strong men, with weapon in hand; women and elders, encouraging the brave that march to the battlefield."[47] The piece conveys a widespread position within the LM. In the extended address to women in 1910 Ricardo Flores Magón similarly wrote, "[m]ake your husbands, your brothers, your fathers, your sons, and your male friends take up a rifle."[48]

In a later fictional piece entitled "El Triunfo de la Revolución Social" (The Triumph of the Social Revolution), He presented his vision of revolutionary success through a Mexican couple's responses to broader events. The husband foolishly expects improvements from Carranza while the wife holds to the PLM line that meaningful change cannot come through political reshuffling. Eventually they both actively join the anarchist army. At the barricades, Magón describes the division of labor as follows: "[t]he women dig ditches; the men clean their rifles; the children distribute outfits to those champions of the proletariat."[49] Despite the wife's greater militancy and understanding in this story, only her husband levels a weapon against the oppressors. Such idealized gender roles were an important revolutionary goal for the party.

In stark contrast, Ricardo Flores Magón's rhetorical treatment of Margarita Ortega presents an almost opposite view of appropriate women's labor in conducting the revolution. Ortega's story turns the notion of women convincing men to pick up the

---

[46] Robert McKee Irwin. (2003) *Mexican Masculinities*. Minneapolis: University of Minnesota Press, pp. 59-71.

[47] "Hay, pues, que luchar contra el depostimo, y cada quien tiene que luchar según su sexo y edad: los hombres fuertes, con el arma al brazo; las mujeres y los ancianos, animando á los bravos á que marchen al campo de batalla." Unattributed. (1907) "El Deber de la Mujer." *Revolución*, July 6, 1907, p. 1.

[48] "Haced que vuestros esposos, vuestros hermanos, vuestros padres, vuestros hijos y vuestros amigos tomen el fusil." Ricardo Flores Magón (1910). "A La Mujer." *Regeneración*, September 24, 1910; translated by Mitchell Cowen Verter in Chaz Bufe & Mitchell Cowen Veter, Eds. (2005) *Dreams of Freedom: A Ricardo Flores Magón Reader*. Oakland, California: AK Press, p. 236.

[49] "Las mujeres hacen hilas; los hombres limpian sus rifles; los niños reparten parque [sic] a aquellos campeones del proletariado." Ricardo Flores Magón. (1915) "El Triunfo de la Revolución Social." *Regeneración*, October 23, 1915; translated by Mitchell Cowen Verter in Chaz Bufe & Mitchell Cowen Veter, Eds. (2005) *Dreams of Freedom: A Ricardo Flores Magón Reader*. Oakland, California: AK Press, p. 326.

rifle on its head. Together with her daughter Rosaura Gortari, Ortega fought in Baja California against the forces of Díaz, Madero, and Huerta with gun in hand. At the end of 1911 after capture by government forces, Magón reported that Ortega said to the notorious Mexican official who held her, "[t]hey will take me Ensenada and shoot me on foot, as a man; but you, traitor, they will shoot you from behind, as a coward."[50]

Ortega survived that dangerous situation but fell at the hands of Victoriano Huerta's soldiers approximately two years later. In a stirring eulogy, Magón described her impressive martial qualities as follows:

> An able horsewoman and an expert in the use of firearms, Margarita crossed the enemy lines and smuggled arms, munitions, dynamite, whatever was needed, to the comrades on the field of action. More than once her boldness and coolness saved her from falling into the clutches of the forces of tyranny. Margarita Ortega had a great heart: from her horse, or from behind a rock, she could shoot down a government soldier, and a little later once could see her caring for the wounded, feeding the convalescents, or providing words of consolation to the widows and orphans. Apostle, warrior, nurse – this exceptional woman was all of these simultaneously.[51]

When compared with other PLM expressions the proper place of women in the struggle—many earlier, some later—this account represents a decided queering of gender roles. Ortega was not just a combatant but an outstanding one. The reversal becomes even more obvious when the article recounts Ortega's break with her husband's conservatism. Ricardo Ortega expresses the matter in explicitly gendered terms: "I'm resolved to continue fighting for the cause of the Partido Liberal Mexicano, and if you're a man, come with me to the battle. If that's not the case, forget me; I don't want to be the partner of a coward."[52] Ortega followed Magón's

---

[50] "[…] me llevarán á Ensenada y me fusilarán de pie, como á un hombre; pero á tí, traidor, te matarán por la espalda, como á un cobarde." Ricardo Flores Magón. (1911) "¡Basta!" *Regeneración*, September 9, 1911, p. 2.

[51] "Hábil ginete y experta en el manejo de las armas del fuego, Margarita atravezaba las líneas enemigas y conducía armas, parque, dinamita, lo que se necesitaba, a los compañeros en el campo de la acción. Más de una vez, su arrojo y su sangre fría la salvaron de caer en las garras de las fuerzas de la tiranía. Margarita Ortega tenía un gran corazón: desde su caballo, o detrás de un peñasco, podía tener a raya a los soldados del gobierno, y poco después podíase verla cuidando a los heridos, alimentando a los convalecientes o prodigando palabras de consuelo a las viudas y a los huérfanos. Apóstol, guerrera, enfermera, todo a la vez era esta mujer excepcional." Ricardo Flores Magón. (1914) "Margarita Ortega." *Regeneración*, June 13, 1914, p. 6; translated by Mitchell Cowen Verter in Chaz Bufe & Mitchell Cowen Veter, Eds. (2005) *Dreams of Freedom: A Ricardo Flores Magón Reader.* Oakland, California: AK Press, p. 228.

[52] "Estoy resuelta a seguir luchando por la causa del Partido Liberal Mexicano, y si eres hombre, vente conmigo a la campaña; de lo contrario, olvídame, pues yo no quiero ser la compañera de un cobarde." Ricardo Flores Magón. (1914) "Margarita Ortega." *Regeneración*, June 13, 1914, p. 6; translated by Mitchell Cowen Verter in Chaz Bufe & Mitchell Cowen Veter, Eds. (2005) *Dreams of Freedom: A Ricardo Flores Magón Reader.* Oakland, California: AK Press, p. 229.

1910 appeal to women to pressure the men in their lives to fight, but on terms of equality rather than any natural or traditional notion of separate aptitudes and duties. The fact that Magón himself never personally took up the rifle as he urged other men to do and instead served the revolutionary enterprise through his writing further heightens the sense that the idealized gender roles he embraced rhetorically did not necessarily reflect how members of the PLM actually conducted themselves in practice. Various observers—particularly an anarchist paper in France—made a point of criticizing him for not taking to the field in Baja California. This element enhances the internal contradiction.

While the narrative of women as military heroes sharply conflicts with Guerrero's disgust for masculinized women and advocacy of distinct spheres for each sex, it accords with the broader revolutionary artistic and literary trend of exalting manly woman under certain circumstances. A picture emerges of a gender ideology that considered reasonable levels of masculinity laudable in either gender but considered femininity only desirable for women and abhorrent for men. In other cases, Ricardo Flores Magón positively described women as "virile" (*viril*).[53] This exposes the complexity of gender ideology within the PLM and possible differences between Guerrero and Ricardo Flores Magón on the matter. It can also be read as an effort to heighten the sense of shame PLM propagandists believed was an effective motivating tool. Magón likely hoped readers would react to the cowardice of Ortega's husband and her bravery by hoisting a rifle themselves to prove they were in fact true men. In any case, his eulogy suggests a level of fluidity in gender constructions and the acceptability of women adopting traditionally masculine roles as part of the revolutionary project.

A second example of an important distinction in gendered labor emerges in the case of nonexistent or insufficient regular employment. PLM texts consistently refer to larceny as the arena of desperate men, and prostitution as the occupation of desperate women. Like so many anarchist, communist, and socialist groups, the PLM wished to assure everyone the necessities of life with dignified and healthful employment. As such, the party took a firm stance against prostitution, describing it as more of an economic than a moral ill and even attacking marriage as a form of prostitution if contracted for support rather than love. Ricardo Flores Magón expressed this succinctly when he wrote, "[a]sk the prostitute why she sells her body and she will answer you: because I am hungry."[54] The robber—the masculine response to starvation in this construction—provided the same explanation. This contrasts with the condemnatory and dehumanizing attitude expressed by experts and government

[53] For example, see Ricardo Flores Magón. (1911) "Sigue su Curso Natural la Revolucion Economica de Mexico." *Regeneración*, September 16, 1911, p. 1.

[54] "Preguntad á la prostituta por qué vende su cuerpo y os contestará: porque tengo hambre." Ricardo Flores Magón. (1911) "Franciso I. Madero Escupe a la Faz del Proletariado." *Regeneración*, April 22, 1911, p. 1.

official who studied and wrote about prostitution in the same period. The motivations they ascribed to prostituted women center on vice rather than need.[55]

Magón identified sexual exploitation as a key element of oppression that motivated his revolutionary action against the existing social order. In a 1909 letter, he described how a Díaz official offered to pay him off to betray the revolution. During this process, the following called him back to the cause: "I thought about the laborers stooped in their work, about the women of the people prostituted by the masters; I thought about the nakedness of those who worked, about the neglect of humble families, about the desperation of the women raped by the soldiery of the Caesar [Porfirio Díaz]."[56] Near the end of his life, Magón wrote to a friend from prison. For the purpose of constructing himself a victim of political repression he made a list of the crimes he was innocent of that included "I have not exploited women's prostitution."[57] Though not above employing—metaphorically and otherwise—the trope of the repulsive whore, Magón and the PLM in general put forth a view of sex work that was dramatically different from the mainstream Díaz-era position and closer to the post-revolutionary reformers of the 1920s Bliss describes in *Compromised Positions*. Among revolutionary soldiers, Bliss shows a prevalent cult of masculinity that lauded or at least tolerated acquiring sex through economic power. This model of masculinity makes no appearance whatsoever in PLM literature. The ideal party man pursued reproductive heterosexual partnership on the nominal basis of equality.[58]

Taken as a whole, these PLM positions on gender identity and expression combined emancipatory rhetoric with a restrictive narrative of naturalness that pathologized deviation. Neither the emancipatory rhetoric nor the narrative of naturalness completely dominated the discourse. PLM writers consistently brought up both the oppression of women and their need for liberation but couched this vision with set gender roles. Assertive masculinity came to be the desired national and/or revolutionary performance, thus allowing positive masculinization for women in certain cases but casting effeminacy in men with all the worst traits of the old regime and of capitalism as well. For PLM writers, discursively employing the popular trope of the passive homosexual transvestite as the antithesis of revolutionary masculinity must have seemed obvious and unproblematic.

---

[55] Katherine Elaine Bliss. (2001) Compromised Positions: Prostitution, Public Health, and Gender Politics in Revolutionary Mexico City. University Park: Penn State Press, pp. 23-46.

[56] "Pensé en los peones encorvados en su trabajo, en las mujeres del pueblo prostituidas por los amos; pensé en la desnudez de los que trabajan, en el desamparo de las familias humildes, en la desesperación de las mujeres violadas por la soldadezca del César." Letter to Elizabeth Trowbridge Sarabia, February 21, 1909 in Ricardo Flores Magón. *Correspondencia*, vol 1. Mexico City: Consejo Nacional para la Cultura y las Artes, pp. 511-512.

[57] Letter to Erma Barsky, March 16, 1922 in Ricardo Flores Magón. *Correspondencia, Vol 1*. Mexico City: Consejo Nacional para la Cultura y las Artes, pp. 348.

[58] Katherine Elaine Bliss. (2001) *Compromised Positions: Prostitution, Public Health, and Gender Politics in Revolutionary Mexico City*. University Park: Penn State Press, pp. 23-46.

References

Albro, Ward S. (1992) *Always a Rebel: Ricardo Flores Magón and the Mexican Revolution.* Fort Worth: Texas Christian University Press.

Bliss, Katherine Elaine. (2001) *Compromised Positions: Prostitution, Public Health, and Gender Politics in Revolutionary Mexico City.* University Park: Penn State Press.

Bufe, Chaz., & Mitchell Cowen Veter, Eds. (2005) *Dreams of Freedom: A Ricardo Flores Magón Reader.* Oakland, California: AK Press.

Domínguez-Ruvalcaba, Héctor. (2007) *Modernity and the Nation in Mexican Representations of Masculinity: From Sensuality to Bloodshed.* New York: Palgrave Macmillan.

Flores Magón, Ricardo. (2000) *Correspondencia, 4 Vols.* Mexico City: Consejo Nacional para la Cultura y lasArtes, México.

Gómez-Quiñones, Juan. (1973) *Sembradores, Ricardo Flores Magón y el Partido Liberal Mexicano: A Eulogy and Critique.* Los Angeles: Aztlán Publications.

Gutmann, Matthew C. (2003) *Changing Men and Masculinities in Latin America.* Duke University Press.

Gutmann, Matthew C. (2007) *The Meanings of Macho: Being a Man in Mexico City.* Berkeley: University of California Press.

Hart, John Mason. (1987) *Revolutionary Mexico: The Coming and Process of the Mexican Revolution.* Berkeley: University of California Press.

Hekma, Gert, Harry Oosterhuis, & James Steakley, Eds. (1995) *Gay Men and the Sexual History of the Political Left.* New York: The Hayworth Press, Inc..

Irwin, Robert McKee. (2003) *Mexican Masculinities.* Minneapolis: University of Minnesota Press.

Kissack, Terence. (2008) *Free Comrades: Anarchism and Homosexuality in the United States 1895-1917.* Oakland: AK Press.

Knight, Alan. (1986) *The Mexican Revolution. 2 Vols.* Lincoln: University of Nebraska Press.

MacLachlan, Colin M. (1991) *Anarchism and the Mexican Revolution: The Political Trials of Ricardo Flores Magón in the United States.* Berkeley: University of California Press.

Olcott, Jocelyn, Mary K. Vaughan, & Gabriela Cano, Eds. (2006) *Sex in Revolution: Gender, Politics and Power in Modern Mexico.* Duke University Press.

Pérez, Emma. (1999) *The Decolonial Imaginary: Writing Chicanas into History.* Bloomington: University of Indiana Press.

Pilcher, Jeffrey M., Ed. (2003) *The Human Tradition in Mexico.* Wilmington, Delaware; SR Books.

Sandos, James A. (1992) *Rebellion in the Borderlands: Anarchism and the Plan of San Diego, 1904-1923.* Norman, University of Oklahoma Press.

Scott, Joan Wallach. (1999) *Gender and the Politics of History.* New York: Columbia University Press.

Suárez Findlay, Eileen J. (1999) *Imposing Decency: The Politics of Sexuality and Race in Puerto Rico, 1870-1920.* Durham: Duke University Press.

Turner, Ethel Duffy. (1984) *Ricardo Flores Magón y el Partido Liberal Mexicano*. Ciudad México: Comisión Nacional Editorial del C.E.N.

El Popular (Mexico City), 1901

Regeneración (Mexico City), 1900-1901

Regeneración (San Antonio, Texas), 1904-1905

Regeneración (St. Louis, Missouri), 1905-1906

Regeneración (Los Angeles, California), 1910-1918

Revolución (Los Angeles, California), 1907-1908

.

3

Graphic Representations of Grammatical Gender in Spanish Language Anarchist Publications

Mariel M. Acosta Matos*

In the last few decades, particularly after social movements in the 1970s, new ways to mark grammatical gender in the Spanish language have emerged to challenge the normative ones. This essay is an initial effort to describe and analyze the ways anarchists subvert the grammatical norms of standard Spanish in written language in their publications. Anarchists eliminate the common morphemes that mark grammatical gender (*-a* and *–o*) in Spanish and substitute them with what I, for now, call Graphic Alternatives to Grammatical Gender (GAGG), the graphic symbols: @, /, = and the letters *-x* and *–e*, turning words like *compañeras* (fem) and *compañeros* (masc) into *compañerxs*, *compañer@s*, etc., creating expressions with neutral or ambiguous grammatical-gender markers that are used with the purpose of eliminating the binary gender morphology. Examples of the GAGG were drawn from articles in the anarchist contemporary self-published (Do It Yourself) journals *Acción Directa* (Perú), *Organización Obrera* (Argentina) and *El Amanecer* (Chile).

This kind of linguistic practice has been penetrating mainstream discourses for many years now. One may see nowadays in various kinds of texts, and in different registers, the use of the @ symbol and the *-x*, in writings by other radicals (LGBTQI), social justice activists, in mainstream media and institutions, and even by individuals not affiliated with a political group. For example, you may see the spelling Latin@ in Latin American/Latino Studies departments and programs in several universities across the country, as well as in advertisements, signs, banners, and other mediums of written Spanish language. Given the apparent normalization of many of the GAGG (particular @ and *–x*) I am particularly interested in analyzing their use in anarchist publications, the context in which they occur in a text, and their rhetorical and stylistic use.

This paper offers a descriptive analysis of these graphic alternatives. I will begin by discussing the grammatical rules of expressing gender in Spanish, and will briefly summarize ongoing debates concerning "linguistic sexism" in Spanish. Then I will present some examples of the GAGG drawn from articles found in 3 "Do It Yourself" journals published online by three anarchist collectives in Latin America.

* Mariel M. Acosta Matos holds a BA in Anthropology from Hunter College and an MA in Spanish from the City College in New York. Her research interests include: the intersections of language, gender, and sexuality; early articulations of Dominican anarchism as well as the turn-of-the-century transnational dimension of Latin American and Spanish Caribbean anarchism. She has given guest lectures, presentations, and workshops on anarchism in the Dominican Republic and her work on anarchist's subversion of Spanish language grammatical gender norms. Currently, Mariel spends most of her time caring for her awesome baby Sandino and she continues conducting her research on the history of anarchism in the Dominican Republic and on gender neutral linguistic strategies against dominant linguistic sexism and androcentrism.

Cover of *Acción Directa* (Perú). Grupo Acción Directa (2011). *Acción Directa*, vol 1 no.1: pp. 1-9.

Finally, I will explain how the GAGG have other rhetorical purposes, beyond extending solidarity to non-binary people. In some contexts, the GAGG allow the speaker or writer to align themselves or establish solidarity with others. This becomes evident in nouns such as "workers," "comrades," "friends," and "neighbours," as well as in pronouns like *nosotrxs* ("us") and *todxs* ("we,") as in picture 1. Simultaneously, the GAGG allows the author to establish a separation from or a relation of opposition toward enemy entities (such as police, guards, and lawyers) for whom the masculine grammatical gender is maintained.

The phrase in this cover (*Acción Directa: Todxs llevamos un policía dentro. Acábalo!* [We all have a cop inside. Finish him!]) is similar to 'kill your inner fascist' and 'kill your inner cop'. The phrase alludes to the Foucauldian notion of panopticsim: how people have been conditioned to police themselves and others and how the prison system extends beyond prison walls, penetrates our minds and pits us against each other. The phrase *Todxs*-GAGG-PL *llevamos*, in which the *–x* is used as alternative, contrasts with *un*-MASC *policía*-NEUT Acábalo-MASC, which maintains the masculine grammatical gender marker *–o*. This idea will be further developed in the last section of this paper.

Anarchist Publications in Latin America

In most Latin American countries where anarchist ideas and people have had a presence, the press has been one of the main platforms for the dissemination of ideas and information – both at the local level and internationally – since the XIX century. The DIY production and distribution of journals, newspapers, zines and other kinds of periodicals is a part of anarchist economic practice, as they are non-commercial and (relatively) small circulation texts. These publications are produced horizontally by a collective and without a motive to make a profit. As Portwood-Stacer puts it, buying or exchanging DIY-produced media (as well as other products) is an anti-consumption practice, which "[signifies] an opposition to the kinds of lifestyles encouraged by the bourgeois consumer culture" (2013: 27). In fact, the journals analyzed in this paper are distributed for free on the websites of the collectives that produce them and are available in print by donation or at cost price. In its covers *Acción Directa* indicates that the suggested contribution for the newspaper is 50 cents of Nuevo Sol (Peruvian currency equivalent to $0.15 USD), *Organización Obrera* costs 2 Argentinean pesos (about $0.20 USD) and *El Amanecer* charges by donation. These publications are also distributed at anarchist book fairs, concerts, talks and other events, as well as in radical bookstores, independent distros and infoshops.

The publications I focused on for this research are just three of over a hundred DIY newspapers and journals in Spanish that are currently published both in print and digital format by anarchist collectives in Latin America, Spain and the US. In a 2014 article "Prensa (A) en América Latina," an updated version of the 2012 article "El retorno de la prensa (A) en América Latina," in the Venezuelan anarchist newspaper

Title	El Amanecer by Grupo el Amanecer Anarquista	Acción Directa by Grupo Acción Directa	Organización Obrera by Federación Obrera Regional Argentina (F.O.R.A)
Country	Chile	Perú	Argentina
Vol. Num. (Year)	1.1 (2011) 2.7 (2012) 3.23 (2013)	1.1 (2011) 2.4 (2012) 3.5 (2013)	8.23 (2009) 10.33 (2011) 12.40 (2013-2014)
Length	8 pp. 8 pp. 8 pp.	9 pp. 9 pp. 9 pp.	12 pp. 12 pp. 12 pp.

Table 1. List of analyzed publications.

El Libertario, indicates that by 2014 there were 100 active anarchist publications, an increase from the 66 they accounted for in their earlier (2012) research. These numbers include Brazilian publications but do not include publications from Spain or the US. Our own update of those numbers indicates that as of 2015, there are currently 106 active anarchist publications in print and online that circulate in Latin America. The newspapers and journals in *El Libertario*'s list publish articles covering a range of topics, including animal liberation, eco-activism, feminist and queer issues, labor movements, indigenous resistance, and anarchist histories from the US, Europe, and Latin American. They also include opinion-based articles and contributions by readers.

This paper examines written discourse data drawn from 21 articles published in three journals. The first, *El Amanecer* from Chile, is currently not editing new issues. However, the website is still maintained and articles and updates continue to be published. The second, *Organización Obrera*, has circulated since 2001 and is published by the Federación Obrera Regional de Argentina (F.O.R.A.) [Argentine's Regional Workers' Federation] founded over a century ago in 1901. And lastly, *Acción Directa* from Perú, was first published in 2011 after the "rebirth" of the collective of the same name. These publications contain articles where some of the GAGG are used in various contexts. The author(s) of most of the articles in these publications are either not identified, identified as "anonymous," or identified with pseudonyms that serve to conceal the person's identity.

An analysis of Latin American anarchists' media, whether fanzines, newspapers, journals, magazines, or any form of online publication, provides insight into their discourses and actions. These texts serve to disseminate ideas, histories, events, and chronicles of actions and confrontations with the police and/or military, as well as other state entities. These non-uniform and anti-authoritarian "guerilla" texts combat normalized anti-authoritarian systems of textual production that are often compromised by capitalist, patriarchal, heteronormative, racist, etc. values (Jeppesen, 2010: 473). These texts provide alternative or "parallel discursive arenas" where, as Fraser asserts, members of subordinate social groups create and circulate discourses [...] that allow them to formulate oppositional interpretations of their identities, interests and needs" as an alternative to bourgeois hegemonic domination of the public sphere (as quoted in Petra, 2001: 16).

Spanish Language Rules for Expressing Grammatical Gender

Grammatical gender is one of the many systems used to classify nouns and can vary from language to language. In most cases, grammatical gender in Spanish is a morphosyntactic category. Nouns, determiners (incld. quantifiers, possessives, articles, and demonstratives), adjectives, pronouns and passive participles belong to either feminine or masculine grammatical gender classes (Bengoechea 2011: 37) and elements that form sentences and phrases generally agree in gender.

When we study the gender morphemes in Spanish, we distinguish between "natural gender," which marks nouns with animate referents (human or animals) based on their perceived sex (masculine/feminine), and "artificial gender," which marks the grammatical gender of inanimate referents (Wheatley, 2006: 76). I will only focus on the natural gender category with human referents. Kathleen Wheatley (2005: 76-78) identifies five basic patterns in standard Spanish to express grammatical gender (see Table 2).

At the lexical level, grammatical gender is defined by the binary opposition of lexical items:

(1) in pairs of different words, such as, *padre / madre*, 'father / mother;' *yerno / nuera*, 'son-in-law / daughter-in-law'

At the morphosyntactic level the distinction of gender is based on:

(2) the use of same radical with different masculine or feminine gender morpheme: *heroe/heroína*, 'hero/heroine.' In some pairs of words, the feminine forms are more often a derogatory term as compared to the masculine: *zorro* 'fox' and *zorra* (synonymous with slurs such as slut or prostitute, similar to the connotation of 'bitch' in English).

(3) the morpheme *–o* for masculine and *-a* for the feminine: *hijo / hija* 'son / daughter'

(4) the consonant ending for the masculine noun or adjective: *-n*, *-s* and *–r* and that is feminized by adding the *-a* morpheme: *señor / señora* 'mister / miss,' *portugués / portuguesa* 'Portuguese' and *peatón / peatona* 'pedestrian'

In this last category, it is evident that the masculine grammatical gender marker is the 'unmarked' element of the pair, which makes it the 'default' gender (Bengoechea, 2011: 37).

In standard Spanish, grammatical gender is not always marked in the morphological structure of given nouns. In such cases, gender is marked by other parts of the constituent: the determiner or the adjectives. In these cases, gender is indicated at the syntactic level:

(5) el atleta cubano / la atleta cubana
    'The-MASC Cuban-MASC atlete' / 'The-FEM Cuban-FEM atlete'

This example further illustrates grammatical gender agreement or concord between the parts of speech.

	Lexical	Morphosyntactic
Binary opposites	padre / madre	
Masculine form as generic	el hombre	los alumnos buenos
Common noun / Gender in determiners and modifiers		el atleta cubano / la atleta cubana
Gender-marked morphemes		
-o (m) / -a (f)		hijo / hija
-e (m) / -a (f)		héroe / heroína | jefe / jefa
-n, -s, -r (m) / -a (f)		peatón / peatona / portugués / portuguesa / señor / señora

Table 2. Prepared by the author based on: Bengoechea, Mercedes (2011). "Non-sexist Spanish Policies: an attempt bound to fail?" *Current Issues in Language Planning.* Vol. 12, no.1: pp. 37; Wheatley, Kathleen (2006). *Sintaxis y morfología de la lengua española.* New Jersey: Prentice Hall, pp. 76-78.

A sixth category that should be added to Wheatley's model is the use of the masculine form as epicene, unmarked or generic form, such as *hombre* 'man' to refer to a collective regardless of the gender identities of its members. The masculine form as generic is used to encapsulate both the feminine and masculine gender categories. According to the norms of use of grammatical gender in Spanish, regardless of the position of enunciation of the speaker (either masculine, feminine or non-binary) and the referents, the group or collective should be expressed in the masculine grammatical form; this form, according to Bengoechea, alienates women (2015: 4): and it alienates and 'erases' non-binary identifying people.

Mainstream Challenges to Linguistic Sexism in Spanish Language

The norms that prescribe grammatical gender in Spanish reflect the androcentric use of language. Other linguists name this form of discrimination "linguistic sexism," which consists of the unequal "distribution of linguistic practices centered on the predominance of the [masculine] grammatical gender based on ideological motivations of the cultural and traditional kind" (Cabeza Pereiro y Rodríguez Barcia, 2013: 8). As mentioned before, in standard Spanish the masculine form (either lexical or morphological) is the unmarked form imposed by prescriptive grammar. This rule is safeguarded and enforced by the *Real Academia de la Lengua Española* (RAE) [Royal Academy of Spanish Language], founded in the XVII Century. The RAE has affiliate institutions and branches in most Spanish-speaking countries around the world, including the Philippines and the United States, and publishes dictionaries, manuals, and orthographies that prescribe the grammatical rules of the language. In fact, the RAE even condemns the use of doublets, such as *profesor y profesora* in a sentence and suggests the use of the masculine form is generic/inclusive.

In the last four decades, the rejection to linguistic sexism and the demand for the "visibility of women" (Bengoechea, 2011: 37; Cabeza Pereiro and Rodríguez Barcia, 2013: 8) in language has risen and the sexist features of standard Spanish have been widely contested in various spheres such as government institutions (places of employment, ministries and institutes) and civil society (academia, NGOs, job places, syndicates etc) in Spain and in Latin America. Institutions and organizations have published manuals that address androcentrism in language, women's erasure from language, instructional discrimination based on gender, patriarchy, sexism, and other issues. Generally, the aim of these institutions is to educate the public and promote the inclusion of women within discourse in mainstream spaces.

This resource of making language inclusive for women is known as "feminization of language" (Pauwels, 1998, 2003; Abbou, 2011, 2013; Scott, 1986, 2010). However, this "language planning initiative" (Bengoechea, 2011: 37-8) still maintains the grammaticality of Spanish and the masculine/feminine binary morphology. Most, if not all, of the suggestions involve the introduction of the feminine morphological marker, *-a* in otherwise "masculine" words, such as names or occupation like *abogada* or *presidenta* that would otherwise be used in the masculine (Bengoechea, n.d: 16-17); the use of doublets, such as *compañeros* (m) *y compañeras* (f); or the use of epicenes, such as "people" instead of "men" or "man" for a collective. The feminization of language does not satisfy the discursive needs of all speakers, particularly LGBT or gender-queer identifying people; it excludes those who do not identify with either one of the binary gendered forms of address. As opposed to these mainstream institutions and organizations, anarchists do not seek validation or recognition from the state or its state institutions. They do not seek to uphold the conventions of language and grammar. Anarchists look to explore and expand the possibilities of expression that language provides, rather than to propose or conform to liberal reforms of language.

Anarchist Prefigurative Politics and Language Planning

In this broader debate concerning sex and gender discrimination in Spanish, anarchists' antisexist linguistic practices and language planning initiatives emerge. Anarchists' use of GAGG constitutes a micro-level language planning practice which in Liddicoat and Baldauf's sense is "located in the work of individuals or small groups of individuals" (Liddicoat & Baldauf, 2008: 5). Anarchist models are implemented by social justice groups, communities, and like-minded people, etc., as opposed to being implemented by institutions and states. Anarchists have also advanced discourses on using GAGG, emphasizing GAGG's importance and political implications. In the case of anarchist individuals and collectives, these micro-level language planning practices materialize when: (1) there is an understanding of the relation of unequal social gender relations and other forms of oppression and their manifestation in language, which leads to (2) meta-pragmatic discourses on sexism in language that circulate in blogs, articles, and statements published to explain their understanding of sexism in language, and (3) changing binary and the masculine-centered linguistic forms in publications.

The deliberate alteration of language for political purposes is an aspect anarchists' "prefigurative politics" (Cohn, 2015; Breton et al., 2012; Heckert, 2006): that is, the practice of enacting (in the present) the society envisioned in the future, thus making 'utopia' real (Peggy Kornegger, 1996: 166). Through their overall praxis of challenging and transforming traditional gender roles and relations, anarchists prefigure a more egalitarian society, and with the use of GAGG they seek to reflect this possibility in language. And, as Jesse Cohn states, through a prefigurative form of organization anarchist resistance culture seeks to "embody the idea in the act, the principle in the practice, the end in the means" (2015: 16-17). In other words, anarchists' prefigurative politics mirrors their desired future through present actions.

Similarly, the challenging and transformation of language for political purposes also relates to the social relations and relations of production that anarchism seeks to destroy and negate; the urge to end domination, smash power over others and destroy the means through which workers are robbed and exploited. And it also relates to anarchists' generative politics reflected in their creative urge (Daring et al., 2012: 7-8), which means that within destruction there is also the possibility for building. Anarchists' urge to destroy manifests in anarchists' treatment of language when they work to dismantle the way the binary categories of sex and gender are maintained and used. They achieve this by adopting forms already in use (the @ symbol, -x, *) or by coming up with new ways of expressing non-binary gender identities (–e, the slash symbol or the equal sign). This dialectical dynamic between destruction and creation destabilizes linguistic and social normativity as we know it and gives way to new ways of expressing erased and oppressed identities. In effect, GAGG formations index the ideologies of anarchists who use them in their publications: as linguistic (and non-linguistic) forms, they represent the users' sociocultural and political conceptions of gender within language.

Anarchists' graphic alternatives to the gender-marking morphemes in Spanish (the @ Symbol and the X)

1.   the @ symbol

The @ symbol began to be used in Spain in the 1970s in the writings of radical left groups and in alternative magazines like *Ajoblanco* (Bengoechea, 2009: 33). Its use has expanded beyond informal texts and alternative press publications, both in print and in online communications/publications. Several institutional manuals and guides, present use of the @ symbol as an alternative; however, they maintain the traditional boundaries of grammatical norms and suggest the use of the @ symbol should go beyond informal interpersonal communications. This contrasts well-produced manuals and guides published by anarcho-syndicalist unions, which identify the use of @ as a GAGG.

Once the use of @ as a GAGG began permeating mainstream spaces and discourses, he RAE intervened against it. In the *Diccionario panhispánico de dudas*, RAE indicates that to avoid "tricky" repetitions that the "recent and unnecessary" custom of alluding to both sexes (in doublets like *los niños y las niñas*) has produced, "[…] the @ symbol has begun to be used in signs and flyer as a graphic resource to integrate in one word the masculine and feminine forms of a noun, given that this sign seems to include in its structure the vowels *a* and *o*: *l@s niñ@s*" (n.p.). The explanation continues with the assertion that because the @ is not a linguistic symbol it should not be used as such, given that it would produce non-viable expressions from a normative point of view. Besides, according to RAE, in phrases like *Día del niñ@*, where the contraction *del* (de + el) is only valid for the masculine, the @ produces a "grave inconsistency" or a lack of agreement in the gender-marking morphemes. Here it becomes clear that the Academy not only condemns the use of non-linguistic symbols like the @ but also condemns the practice of feminizing the language because it affects the economy of the language and the masculine form serves the function of encompassing everyone.

Picture 2. Poster in solidarity with two political prisoners in Chile where the @ symbol is used in *compañe@s* 'comrades' and *pres@s* 'prisoners.' El Amanecer (2012). *Libertad a l@s compañe@s pres@s.* Chile: Grupo El Amanecer.

Of the three newspapers analyzed, *Organización Obrera* deployed the least linguistic alternatives and the @ was most frequently used. The @ is used in phrases such as *comité de ciudadan@s* ('citizen's committee'); *l@s trabajador@s* ('the workers'); and *sus trabajador@s* ('their workers'). The following example is from an article by *Duvrobsky* about Bulgarian women's labor migration to Greece and the forms of discrimination that they face. The article also describes an attack perpetrated against the president of the domestic workers' syndicate: "[...] los derechos de sus trabajador@s, **mayoritariamente mujeres**...la mayoría de **ellas** inmigrantes," "[...] the rights of their workers-GAGG, mostly women [...] most of them-FEM immigrants-NEUT" (March-April 2009: 7). Here the author uses the @ in *trabajador@s* but needs to clarify that the majority of them are ***women***, and reiterates it with the third person deictic pronoun ***ellas,*** which is in gender agreement with the antecedent. The point of this example is to highlight the author's strategies of using the @ symbol to express the gender neutrality of the collective *trabajadora@s* ('workers') while using the pronoun *ellas* ('them') when there is a need to specify the gender of a part of the group. Examples from *Acción Directa* include: "*micrófono abierto* [...] *usado por tod@s*" ("open mic [...] used by everyone-GAGG-PL"), "[...] *dedicado para l@s rebeldes que se encuentran sol@s,*" ("[...] dedicated to the-GAGG-PL rebels that are alone-GAAG-PL"). As mentioned above, this alternative is also widely used in mainstream forms of communication, most likely due to its similarity to a juxtaposed *-a* and *–o*. However, even if its form seems to only allude to male and female referents simultaneously, there is no consensus as to that meaning; therefore the @ is arguably a symbol used to express ambiguity. In terms of its pronunciation, since the @ symbol is not a linguistic sign and there is no vowel or consonant sound associated with it, suggested pronunciations for it include *–oa / -oas, compañeroas.*

2.   The X

–x is another GAGG, in this instance used to substitute for the gender morphemes *–a* and *–o*. X has also been used to extend solidarity with LGBTQI collectives and individuals, because it clearly expresses neither a masculine nor a feminine form (Bengoechea, 2015: 7). The use of the *-x* adds more ambiguity to the identity of the referent, especially compared to @. This alternative expands the possibilities of identification to those whose identities don't fit the feminine and masculine binary and allows writers to not undesired gender identities to anyone.

Picture 3. Banner reads: Libertad a **lxs** anarquistas secuestrad**xs** por el estado. Presos – presas a la kalle. "Freedom to the anarchists kidnapped by the state. Prisoners to the street!" Lxs Solidarixs (2011). "ACCIONES. Crónica de una acción libertaria" *El Amanecer* vol. 1 no.1: p. 3

Organización Obrera:
"*¡Ningún cargo a **lxs** detenid**xs**, huelga general!*"
"No charges to the-GAGG-PL detained-GAGG-PL, general strike!"

El Amanecer:
"*nosotr**xs** somos **lxs** unic**xs**"
"we-GAGG-PL are the-GAGG-PL only ones-GAGG-PL"

"*[...] tod**xs** **lxs** ciudadan**xs** [...]*"
"[...] all-GAGG-PL the-GAGG-PL citizens-GAGG-PL"

Acción Directa:
"*[...]libertad a **lxs** compañer**xs** en $hile [...]*"
"freedom to the-GAGG-PL comrades-GAGG-PL in $hile"

"*[...] **lxs** 14 compañer**xs** anarquistas detenid**xs**"
"The-GAGG-PL 14 detained-GAGG-PL anarchist comrades-GAGG-PL"

3. The use of the slash /

The slash is used to separate the root, or unmarked masculine form, from the feminine morpheme in indefinite articles or nouns. It is used in the same sentence with the –x as we can see in this example from *Acción Directa*:

"*Escrito por **un/a** anónim**x**"
"Written by an-MASC/FEM anonymous-GAGG"

We also found it in other phrases such as "Seré **un/a** encapuchad**x** de este 2012" (April 2012: 3) from an article submitted to *El Amanecer* anonymously via email. For the sake of anonymity, the person who wrote this statement used the slash to add the feminine morpheme to the unmarked/masculine indefinite pronoun "un" (some people would do *unx*) and paired it with the use of *–x* in the noun, *encapuchadx* making the position of enunciation, the "I", ambiguous or non-binary. The use of the GAGG together with the slash that marks both grammatical genders makes these phrases more heterogeneous. Even if a GAGG is accompanied by semi-normalized or more accepted forms (like the slash) these sentences are also transgressive. The use of the slash is not standardized yet: therefore it is not seen as grammatical. The use of a GAGG also asserts inclusiveness and adds to the many possibilities of expressing inclusive gender forms.

A Brief Note on the GAGG's Verbal Articulation

The GAGGs pose a challenge in their verbal articulation, as some are non-linguistic symbols and others are consonants that are substituting a vowel: @, *, x, =, etc. What manner of pronunciation do GAGG's proponents and users suggest? Given that I focus on the analysis of written data, a brief discussion of non-orthographic symbols and pronunciation is pertinent. The X, orthographic symbol with a consonant sound forms various combinations of consonant clusters when being added as a suffix to form *–xs, -rxs, -nxs, -gxs*, as opposed to forming syllables (combinations of vowel and consonant sounds). In Spanish, the pronunciation of the letter *X* in some words is 'ks', as in *conexión* (or words like *axe* in English); therefore, the first kind of combination would be harder to articulate. Spanish has a certain number of consonant sound sequences, but neither include the ones mentioned above.

Some suggest pronouncing *–x* with utilizing the phonetic value of the Spanish letter *J* (the velar voiceless fricative /x/) in words like *ojo* (and *Bach* and *loch* in English). Others have suggested pronouncing *–x* in accord with its phonetic value in Mayan languages: /ʃ/ or 'sh', as in Xicanx (pronounced *Shi-kan-sh*). When the x only appears at the end of a word, as in Chicanx, it could alternatively be pronounced *Chi-kan-ex* (Ramirez, 2008: 5). The fact that Nahuatl and the Mayan languages do not have grammatical gender classes has also influenced the deployment of gender neutral forms among Latinx and Chicanx activists. The use of *-x* reveals the intersection of race/ethnicity and (grammatical) gender politics: it 'symbolizes' efforts to decolonize language. Adopting and using gender neutral nouns and pronouns reclaims Mesoamerican activists' Indigenous languages, as their linguistic systems do not conform with grammatical gender as codified in Spanish. Another gender-neutral form has been proposed by Pirexia, an anarchist affinity group formed in 2010 in Spain, which released publications until 2011. In their article "Notas al uso del lenguaje" ["Notes on the Use of Language"], Pirexia reflects on patriarchy, sexism, gender discrimination, and how these forms of discrimination impact on language. The author(s) also examine different GAGGs (including examples I have discussed) and, after explaining various difficulties they pose, suggest the use of *-e*, as in: "**Les trabajadores** aquí **reunides**, queremos manifestar que no vamos a tolerar la explotación a la que estamos *sometides*" (2011: 34). The letter 'e' is used in all their texts to substitute for masculine and feminine grammatical gender markers because of its ease in articulation (given that it already represents a vowel sound in Spanish). In this way the collective deploys a gender-neutral form that is easily pronounced and avoids any issues that pronunciation of @, X, and other graphic symbols may present.

Use of GAGG in Solidarity vs. use of Masculine Gender as in Conflict

These graphic alternatives may seem disorganized or anti-systematic from a normative grammatical perspective. But these changes to the structure of the language are not meant to follow the rules of Spanish grammar: GAGG usage constitutes a political action with specific purposes. Furthermore, in context, these graphic alternatives are a rhetorical weapon allocating positive values to referents such as 'comrades,' 'workers,' 'neighbours,' etc., and, at the same time, introduce negative values to referents such as 'police,' 'guards,' 'lawyers,' etc. Thus, they reinforce separation and opposition between social forces.

In some contexts, particularly in texts about confrontations with police and other contentious entities, anarchists may align in solidarity or affinity by constructing gender neutral expressions referring to one person (*companerx*) or a collective (*lxs compañerxs*) when the referents are in the 3rd person singular and plural. The gender-neutral forms with GAGG are also constructed when the writer/author includes themselves, using self-referential pronouns (*nosotrxs, todxs*).

In addition to Acción Directa's "Todxs llevamos **un** policía adentro. Acábalo!" ('We-GAGG have a cop-MASC inside. Finish **him**!'), there are other examples in *El Amanecer* that illustrate how normative forms of marking gender embody negative values associated with contending or enemy forces, which, in all cases, utilized the masculine morpheme *-o*:

a. "[…] ni nosotr**xs** mism**xs** entendemos […] no podemos ni guardaremos silencio por Nelson Vildósola, el joven de 19 años asesinado en manos de Carabiner**os** tras un 'confuso' incidente […]"

b. "La mejor forma de recordar a tod**xs** l**xs** asesinad**xs** por el Estado, es con lucha contra ese mismo […]"

Examples **a** and **b** are **taken** from an article in *El Amanecer* by Ayelén de la Revuelta (2012: 4) on the killing of a young man by the police in Chillán, Chile. 'A' states: "*nosotrxs mismxs* we-GAGG can't and will not remain silent in the face of the murder of Nelson Vildósola by the *carabineros* police in a 'confusing incident.'" The positioning of enunciation, 'we' combined with GAGG –*xs* establishes an interrelationship between author and reader while alienation from the police is emphasized through the masculine gender marker *-o*, as in *carabineros, los pacos* and *los esbirros* (the last two are synonyms of 'police officer' or 'cop'). Example **b** expands solidarity with those murdered by the state: *todxs lxs asesinadxs*.

c. "[…] constantes intervenciones de **serenos** expulsando a 'no vecin**xs**' de parques"

d. "**los actores** no son más que caras y nombres que resultan ridículos al lado de lo que los medios tratan de expresar"

In examples **c** and **d** the masculine gender marker is used in contrast to –*xs*. In example **c** it refers to *serenos* ('security guards') and, in example **d,** to actors: both are portrayed as puppets of larger oppressive entities. In **c**, the guards are accused of harassing people for loitering in parks in neighborhoods that they allegedly do not belong to. Here "guards" is marked with the masculine grammatical gender form and "non-neighbors" (loiterers) with the GAGG –*xs*. In example **d**, the word "actors," denoting those who participate in hostile commercial propaganda in the media, is also marked with the masculine gender. Here, standard grammatical form suggests a negative identity value associated with cops and actors, as the normative form indexes the regulatory (cultural, linguistic, social and economic) system to which anarchists are opposed.

e. "[…] con ella [la capucha] me igualo a mis *compañerxs* mientras insultamos a *los esbirros* del poder"

Similarly, example **e** expresses affinity and solidarity with comrades using a hood to mask their face (*compañerxs*) and opposition toward the repressive forces (henchmen) of the state (*los esbirros del poder*). The author observes that a hood or mask is a powerful tool of evasion and protest, "[…] because with it I'm protected, because with it I show my hatred, my anger to this violent system." The caption accompanying a related illustration declares: "[t]he hood doesn't hide, it shows!" (2012: 2). Echoing the use of author-pseudonyms and GAGG's gender neutral formations, the hood conceals one's identity in the streets. Here we see how non-verbal style practices complement on-the-ground activism and are a means of 'indexing' identity/ies, affinities, and solidarities.

Una breve reflexión sobre la capucha

recibido al mail,
Escrito por un/a anónimx.

Fui, soy y seré un encapuchadx, taparé mi rostro con esa sudada y ardiente polera, porque con ella estoy protegidx, porque con ella muestro mi odio, mi rabia a este violento sistema, con ella me iguato a mis compañerxs mientras insultamos a los esbirros del poder, ella es mi cómplice cuando rompemos las estructuras capitalistas que nos oprimen y prendemos neumáticos y basura al fuego en medio de la calle, seré un/a encapuchadx de este 2012 y seré el temor de la autoridad y el tema en la mesa de cada familia autoritaria, en la boca de todxs lxs ciudadanxs moralistas que ejercen una pega muy similar a la del paco.

LA CAPUCHA es el ROSTRO DEL PUE... en LA LUCH@

¡LA CAPUCHA NO ESCONDE, MUESTRA!

Picture 4. From the article "Una breve reflexión sobre la capucha" by Un/a anonimx (2012). *El Amanecer* vol. 2 no.7 (April 2012, p.3)

Just as covering one's face to protect oneself simultaneously 'exposes' a person's resistance, so the use of −x and the other gender-neutral alternatives expands the possibilities of enunciation in a given discourse.

Final Thoughts

Using graphic alternatives in language contributes to discussions on discrimination based on sex and gender. These forms radicalize discourses concerning language usage among mainstream and reformist critics of linguistic sexism, who tend to focus, exclusively on the situation of women. These graphic alternatives allow speakers to learn, recognize and acknowledge the multiple possibilities of expression that the Spanish language has had and could possibly have. This is particularly important for non-binary individuals who do not actively signify queerness in their bodies and may be mis-gendered.

Many have criticized the alteration of language as a futile strategy that does not address the issues of gender inequality and discrimination directly and they are mere cosmetic alterations of the language. These critics argue that the focus instead should be on tackling inequality and discrimination that affect people's material conditions and having conversations on heteropatriarchy and gender discrimination. However, if those material changes involve having conversations about these issues, there needs to be a language for engaging in those conversations and the alternative gender categories that have been created by LGBTQI people should not be ignored.

Linguists Susan Ehrlich and Ruth King posit that even if gender-based language reform may not be immediately or completely successful, it "sensitize[s] individuals to ways in which language is discriminatory towards women [and non-binary identifying people]," and therefore demonstrates that "language becomes one of the many arenas where social inequalities are elucidated" (1998: 170). Similarly, as Trevor Pateman points out, "outer changes" such as non-sexist language can affect inner attitudes and, potentially, change the political status quo: "the change in outward practice constitutes a restructuring of at least one aspect of one social relationship […] every act reproduces or subverts a social institution" (as quoted in Cameron, 1985: 172). Mercedes Bengoechea also observes that while non-binary articulations might not have revolutionized social gender relations at present, they enable the visibility of non-binary and queer identities in discourse, and, very importantly, contribute to questioning and destabilization the Spanish language's patriarchal and androcentric grammar (2015: 21).

While GAGG and other changes to language-usage that seek to dissolve male/female binaries – such as English pronouns (ey, ze, xe, they) – have not ended gender discrimination and violence toward transgender and queer people, furthering the discussion of gender discrimination and the linguistic erasure of women and non-binary people contributes to dismantling hegemonic discourses that perpetuate discriminatory ideologies generally, including within anarchist circles.

References

Abbou, Julie. (2011) "Double Gender Marking in French: A Linguistic Practice of Antisexism," *Language Planning*, Vol. 12, no. 1: pp. 55-75.

Arias Barredo, Aníbal. (1990) "Género gramatical y motivación semántica," *Estudios de Lingüística Universidad de Alicante*, Vol. 6: pp. 107-21.

Bengoechea, Mercedes, et al. (2009) *Efectos de las políticas lingüísticas antisexistas y feminización del lenguaje.* Madrid: Instituto de la Mujer.

---. (2011) "Non-sexist Spanish Policies: an attempt bound to fail?" *Current Issues in Language Planning.* Vol 12, no. 1 : pp. 35-53.

---. (2012) *Sexismo y androcentrismo en los textos administrativo-normativos.* Alcalá: Universidad de Alcalá. Web. <http://www.upm.es/sfs/Rectorado/Gerencia/Igualdad/Lenguaje/sexsismo y androcentrismo en textos administrativos.pdf>

---. (2015) "Cuerpos hablados, cuerpos negados y el fascinante devenir del género gramatical." *Bulletin of Hispanic Studies.* Vol. 92, no.1 : pp. 1-23.

---. (n.d.) *Sexismo y androcentrismo en los textos administrativo-normativos.* Alcalá: Universidad de Alcalá. Web. <https://drive.google.com/file/d/0B1OhCa48TcPeNGNOdVFyZkUtVVU/edit_>

Bergvall, Victoria, Janet Bing and Alice Freed, eds. (1996) *Rethinking Language and Gender Research: Theory and Practice.* New York: Longman.

Breton, Émilie, Sandra Jeppesen, Anna Kruzynski and Rachel Sarrasin. (2012) "Prefigurative Self-Governance and Self-Organization: The Influence of Antiauthoritarian (Pro)Feminist, Radical Queer and Antiracist Networks in Quebec." *Organize! Building from the Local Global Justice.* Eds. Aziz Choudry, Jill Hanley and Eric Shragge. Oakland: PM Press, pp. 156-73.

Cabeza Pereiro, María del Carmen y Susana Rodríguez Barcia. (2013) "Aspectos ideológicos, gramaticales y léxicos del sexismo lingüístico." *Estudios Filológicos,* Vol. 52): pp. 7-27. Web. <http://mingaonline.uach.cl/pdf/efilolo/n52/art01.pdf>

Cameron, Deborah. (1985) *Feminism and Linguistic Theory.* New York: St. Martin's Press. Comité Confederal de CGT, Secretariado Permanente y Secretaría de la Mujer (2013). "Manual del lenguaje integrador no sexista." Madrid: Secretaria de Comunicación CGT. Web. <http://www.cgt-cyl.org/IMG/pdf/Manual_no_sexista_definitivo_3_para_web-1.pdf>

Diccionario de la lengua española. 22.ª edición (2001). Madrid, España: Real Academia Española. Web. <http://rae.es/recursos/diccionaios/drae>

Duvrobsky (2009). "Rienda suelta a todas las libertades." *Organización Obrera* Vol. 8, no .23: p. 7

Eckert, Penelope y Sally McConnell-Ginet (2006). *Language and Gender.* Cambridge: University Press.

Ehrlich, Susan and Ruth King (1998). "Gender-Based Language Reform and the Social Construction of Meaning." *The Feminist Critique of Language, 2nd Edition.* Ed. Deborah Cameron. New York: Routledge pp. 164-179.

Federación Obrera Regional Argentina (2009). *Organización Obrera,* Vol. 8, no.23: pp. 1-12.

Federación Obrera Regional Argentina. (2011). *Organización Obrera,* Vol. 10, no .33 : pp. 1-12.

Federación Obrera Regional Argentina. (2013-2014) *Organización Obrera,* Vol. 12, no.40: pp. 1-12.

Grupo Acción Directa (2011). *Acción Directa*, Vol. 1, no .1: pp. 1-9.

Grupo Acción Direct. (2012). *Acción Directa*, Vol. 2, no.4: pp. 1-9.

Grupo Acción Direct. (2013). *Acción Directa*, Vol. 3, no .5: pp. 1-9.

Grupo El Amanecer Anarquista (2011). *El Amanecer*, Vol. 1.1 : pp. 1-8.

Grupo El Amanecer Anarquista. (2012). *El Amanecer*, Vol. 2 no.7: pp. 1-8.

Grupo El Amanecer Anarquista. (2013). *El Amanecer*, Vol. 3 no.23: pp. 1-8.

Grupo Pirexia (2011). "Nota al uso del lenguaje". *Aspectos básicos sobre federalismo anarquista. Organizándonos en libert@d*. Sevilla, España: Grupo anarquista Pirexia.

Instituto Cervantes (2011). "Lo normativo en el uso del género." *Guía de comunicación no sexista*. Madrid:Aguilar, pp. 27-48. Web. <http://www.prisaediciones.com/uploads/ficheros/libro/primeras-paginas/201206/primeras-paginas-gui-comunicacion-no-sexista.pdf>

Jeppesen, Sandra (2009). "Creating Guerilla Texts in Rhizomatic Value-Practices on the Sliding Scale of Autonomy: Toward an Anti-Authoritarian Cultural Logic." *New Perspectives on Anarchism*. Eds. Nathan J. Jun and Shane Wahl. Lanham, MD: Lexington Books: pp. 473-496.

"La institución" *Real Academia Española*. Web. <http://www.rae.es/la-institucion>

Liddicoat, Anthony and Richard Baldauf (2008). "Language Planning in Local Contexts: Agents, Contexts and Interactions" *Language Planning and Policy*. Eds. Anthony J. Liddicoat, Richard B Baldauf Jr. Multilingual Matters Ltd: Buffalo, pp. 3-18.

López de Martínez, Adelaida (1990). "Hacia la emancipación de la lengua por la enseñanza de los géneros gramaticales." *Hispania*, Vol. 73 no. 2: pp. 530-533.

Pauwels, Anne (1998). *Sprache und Geschlecht/Language and Gender* Vol. 1.1,: n.p. Web. <http://www.linguistik-online.com/heft1_99/pauwels.htm>

Scott, Joan W (1986). "Gender: A useful Category of Historical Analysis." *The American Historical Review* Vol. 91 no.5 : pp. 1053-1075.

Scott, Joan W. (2010) "Gender: Still a Useful Category of Analysis?" *Diogenes* Vol. 225. no1: pp. 7-14.

Wheatley, Kathleen (2006). *Sintaxis y morfología de la lengua española*. New Jersey: Prentice Hall.

4.

"A Thought Thinking Itself:"
Post-anarchism in Grant Morrison's *The Invisibles*

Lewis Call*

Grant Morrison's *The Invisibles* (1994-2000) tells the tale of a diverse band of anarchist freedom fighters. Morrison's narrative follows the adventures of a cell within a centuries-old revolutionary organization called the Invisible College. The leader of this cell is King Mob, a bald, pierced fetishist, who resembles Morrison more than a little. Three of King Mob's fellow "Invisibles" present as women: the cross-dressing Brazilian shaman Lord Fanny, a slightly insane time-travelling redhead called Ragged Robin, and an African-American former cop who calls herself Boy. The cell's newest recruit is Jack Frost, a foul-mouthed working-class punk from Liverpool. Together these Invisible revolutionaries fight against an interdimensional authoritarian conspiracy called the "Outer Church." This Outer Church works towards a world in which political, economic and religious institutions unite to create a system of total authority. Meanwhile, the Invisible College works towards the opposite end: a left-libertarian world based upon individual freedom, inclusive diversity, and universal access to the means of happiness (including sex, drugs, and magic). *The Invisibles* can thus be read as an inspirational story of anti-authoritarian rebellion: a strange, beautiful, anarchist fairy tale.

Yet, *The Invisibles* is much more than that. Morrison's comic is also a post-anarchist cultural artifact. Post-anarchism is a radical form of anarchist theory that first emerged in the 1980s. It draws on twentieth century post-structuralism and post-modernism to extend anarchism's critical power beyond its traditional targets, capitalism and the state. Post-anarchism develops powerful critiques of the modern philosophies of subjectivity, sexuality, and semiotics. These critiques permit post-anarchism to deploy a sophisticated revolutionary practice, one which is suitable for use under contemporary conditions. This practice is tactical rather than strategic; it contains a post-anarchist protection against the temptations of large-scale strategic action.

The Invisibles articulates several important post-anarchist ideas. The comic advances a major *anarchy of subjectivity*. This anarchy subverts the modern notion of the stable, autonomous individual, replacing that discredited concept with a post-modern model that understands identity as flexible, fluid, and shifting. This anarchy of subjectivity includes an *anarchy of sexuality* which rejects the concept of sexual "normality" and

* Lewis Call is Professor of History at California Polytechnic State University, San Luis Obispo. He is the author of *Postmodern Anarchism* (Lexington Books, 2002) and *BDSM in American Science Fiction and Fantasy* (Palgrave Macmillan, 2013). He studies post-anarchist themes in popular culture. He has written about post-anarchism in science fiction and fantasy novels (Ursula K. Le Guin, Octavia Butler and Samuel Delany), television shows (*Buffy the Vampire Slayer* and *Battlestar Galactica*), and comic books (*V for Vendetta*). He serves on the editorial boards of *Anarchist Studies* and *Anarchist Developments in Cultural Studies*. He lives in San Luis Obispo with his wife Michelle and their daughter Kate.

emphasizes the liberatory potential of unorthodox sexual subjectivities. Post-anarchism has become known (if not admired) for this interpretive move (Franks, 2007: 130). *The Invisibles* also develops a compelling *anarchy of the symbolic*. The comic warns us of the oppressive power of symbolic language, and shows us how we can resist that power by moving beyond subject-centered language. The ultimate destination of *The Invisibles'* narrative (and of the Invisible revolutionaries who inhabit that narrative) is a purely symbolic realm that has been purged of the language of subjectivity. Morrison calls this realm the Supercontext. The comic examines the era of simulation, a time when life has been thoroughly colonized by the images of the spectacular mass media. The Invisible College uses the techniques of the 1960s Situationists to seize control of simulation and spectacle. Finally, *The Invisibles* develops a post-anarchist critique of dualistic thought. At first Morrison's narrative appears to represent a Manichaean struggle between the forces of authority (Outer Church) and those of freedom (Invisible College). Yet the book slowly subverts its own Manichaean logic. *The Invisibles* ends up promoting an *ontological anarchy* that rejects all dualisms, merging forces that seem fundamentally opposed into the joyful ontological unity of the Supercontext.

"Let's do a Comic Together! Let's Save the World!": Context and Supercontext

Every superhero team has an origin story. This is the origin of the Invisible College. Grant Morrison grew up in a poor working-class family in Glasgow. Morrison notes that he drew on the anti-authoritarianism that comes from growing up poor to create the Jack Frost character (quoted in Meaney, 2011: 313), so Jack is the second Invisible who looks like Morrison. As a teenager, Morrison read "philosophical" comics about magic like *Doctor Strange* (quoted in Meaney, 2011: 340). By the age of 17, he was writing his own comics, for reasons at least partly political. "I was growing up in Thatcher's Britain, and I was desperate," he recalls (quoted in Gunn, 2014: n.p.). In 1988, Morrison was "discovered" by DC Comics, one of the largest American comics publishers. Along with Alan Moore and Neil Gaiman, Morrison was part of the "British Invasion" which took American comics by storm in the 1980s (Hiatt, 2011). Morrison was especially influenced by Moore's *V for Vendetta*, a post-anarchist political fable (see Call, 2008) that Morrison took as a model for the way comics should be (Meaney, 2010). From 1992 on, Morrison says that he was "really involved" with magic, drugs, and weird sex (quoted in Neighly & Cowe-Spigai, 2003: 231). He started dressing like a woman and doing "insane rituals" (Edwards, 2012: 79); the Invisible Lord Fanny was Morrison, too. While Morrison's politics remained generally leftist, his model of political activism became increasingly non-traditional (and specifically post-anarchist). "The best thing to do was just take some Ecstasy and dance, and hope that when you came down […] the Tories would be out," says Morrison (quoted in Hasted, 1995: 79). In 1993, Morrison took his own advice about political action and dropped Ecstasy with comics artist Jill Thompson, who would do some of the best art for *The Invisibles*. Morrison and Thompson went to a rave and said "Hey, let's do a comic together! Let's save the world!" (Morrison quoted in Meaney, 2011: 314).

The Invisibles occupied a very post-anarchist historical moment. Post-anarchism traces its origins to the work of Hakim Bey. In the mid 1980s, Bey introduced the concept of the Temporary Autonomous Zone (TAZ), "a guerilla operation which liberates an area (of land, of time, of imagination) and then dissolves itself to re-form elsewhere/elsewhen" (2003 [1985]: 99). Morrison followed Bey's line of thinking precisely: "I'm not entirely convinced that anarchy as a philosophy is workable, and what *The Invisibles* ultimately deals with is the fact that the human imagination is where freedom is actually contained" (quoted in Hasted, 1995: 82). Speaking about the ideas behind *The Invisibles*, Morrison explicitly invoked the TAZ: "we are owned in certain ways, and we have to find ways to make sort of Temporary Autonomous Zones, as Hakim Bey called it" (quoted in Neighly & Cowe-Spigai, 2003: 38). Interestingly, Bey identified the band or affinity group as the "base unit" of the TAZ (2003 [1985]: 102). For Bey, the band was based on "spiritual affinities" rather than hierarchies, and the band became increasingly important in the "post-Spectacular Society of Simulation" (2003 [1985]: 102). An Invisible cell embodies the band as a model of social organization. Indeed, Bey argued that the greatest strength of the TAZ lay in its *invisibility* (2003 [1985]: 99). The basic premises of Morrison's "Invisiblism" align perfectly with Bey's post-anarchism. Morrison's Invisible revolutionaries routinely take the kind of tactical post-anarchist actions that Bey called for: art-sabotage, ceremonial magic, tantric pornography (2003 [1985]: 58).

In 1994 (the same year *The Invisibles* debuted), Todd May published *The Political Philosophy of Poststructuralist Anarchism*. May described "a new type of anarchism" which rejected "subjectivity as a viable source of political action" and refused to view power as solely repressive (1994: 85). *The Invisibles* shares these rejections and refusals. Saul Newman theorized the anarchy of subjectivity (and brought the term "post-anarchism" to academia) in his 2001 book *From Bakunin to Lacan*. Newman suggested that perhaps revolution should be about escaping subjectivity entirely (2001: 67). Newman employed the theories of the psychoanalyst Jacques Lacan to achieve this escape. In the mid-twentieth century, Lacan had postulated that human reality consisted of the Symbolic (the realm of language and culture), the Real (the realm of unrepresentable experience) and the Imaginary (the realm of image and fantasy). Since the Symbolic is the place of the Law, the Symbolic is a major target for post-anarchism (Call, 2011a: 186-7). *The Invisibles* uses the subversive potential of the visual Imaginary to resist the Symbolic; this is an important implication of Morrison's insight that freedom is located in the imagination. But although the comic undeniably mounts an Imaginary challenge to the Symbolic order, it also shows how the fragmentation of subjectivity can enable a recuperation of the Symbolic.

The anarchy of subjectivity includes a crucial anarchy of sexuality. Newman argues persuasively that the problem of essentialism is *the* political problem of our time (2001: 4). Essentialism is so problematic because it promotes the tyranny of normality (Newman, 2011: 3). Post-anarchism challenges this tyranny by deploying provisional, flexible sexual identities built around alternative sexual practices. Post-anarchist sexuality disrupts essentialist or normalizing forms of sexual identity by endorsing queer and kinky sexualities like LGBTQ, BDSM, fetish, etc (Call, 2011b: 131). These sexualities help to promote post-anarchist ethics and politics (Call,

2011b: 132), e.g. by emphasizing the crucial importance of consent (a fundamental anarchist value). During the 1990s, representations of alternative sexualities like BDSM became increasingly common in American pop culture (Weiss, 2006). This made it easier for Grant Morrison to offer images of revolutionary sexuality in *The Invisibles*. The comic implements post-anarchist sexuality through the fetishism of King Mob, the female dominance of Ragged Robin, and the gay cross-dressing sexuality of Lord Fanny. Morrison says that he "wanted *The Invisibles* to make revolution sexy" (quoted in Neighly & Cowe-Spigai, 2003: 253). To achieve this, he deliberately connected revolutionary politics to the politics of alternative sexuality.

Post-anarchism is centrally concerned with the oppressive power of symbolic language. Many post-anarchists are inspired by the work of Gilles Deleuze and Félix Guattari, who declare that "language is made not to be believed but to be obeyed, and to compel obedience" (1987: 76). For them, language is authoritarian. Nor is revolutionary language immune to power. Lacan notes that "the irony of revolutions is that they engender a power that is all the more absolute in its exercise […] because it is reduced more completely to the words that signify it" (2006: 234). *The Invisibles* represents this irony through the Key drugs, powerful psychoactives, which cause the user to perceive words as the objects they signify. The Key drugs collapse signifier into signified, Symbolic into Real, and so reveal the awful power of language. But *The Invisibles* also represents an important tactic of linguistic liberation. Deleuze and Guattari argue for the revolutionary potential of what they call minor languages, linguistic practices that make dominating languages "minoritarian" (1987: 106). Deleuze and Guattari give women as their main example of a group that speaks minor languages (1987: 106). *The Invisibles* offers the figure of Ragged Robin, a woman author of genre fiction whose minoritarian discourse turns out to be *the narrative of The Invisibles itself*.

By presenting one of its characters as its author, *The Invisibles* argues that there is no fundamental distinction between fiction and reality (Meaney, 2011: 188). Here the comic invokes another major trope of post-anarchism: simulation. Guy Debord and the Situationist International set the stage for the analysis of simulation in the 1960s. Debord defined situationism as "an artistic avant garde" experimenting in "ways for freely constructing everyday life" (Knabb, 2006: 402). The Invisible College is a similar avant garde. Debord called for a revolutionary alteration of culture that would supersede "spectacles separated from life" (Knabb, 2006: 393). In the 1960s – and especially during the revolutionary events of May 1968 – the Situationists launched critical assaults on the Spectacle, on simulation, and on the Symbolic order that made such things possible. They used the *dérive*, "a technique of rapid passage through various ambiences" of psychogeography (Knabb, 2006: 62), in order to make familiar spaces strange. They used *détournement*, "the reuse of preexisting artistic elements in a new ensemble" for revolutionary political purposes (Knabb, 2006: 67). The Invisible College uses both techniques.

"Ragged Robin in the Ganzfeldt Tank."
Art by Chris Weston and Ray Kayssing.

In the 1980s, Jean Baudrillard built upon the work of Debord and the S.I. to create a theory of simulation. Baudrillard argued that the late twentieth century was increasingly a world of simulation, a world in which the distinction between reality and simulation was never clear (if such a distinction existed at all). In the Lacanian model, what we call reality consists of the Real filtered through the Symbolic (Marini, 1992: 46). But in the era of simulation there was *only* the Symbolic. There was no Real for the Symbolic to filter, hence no reality. This era began with the "liquidation of all referentials" (Baudrillard, 1994 [1981]: 2). Baudrillard's world of pure, non-referential simulation might seem to demonstrate, once again, the inexorable tyranny of the Symbolic. Yet simulation theory offers a surprisingly viable revolutionary tactic, for this theory suggests that radical forces could seize the engines of simulation and use those engines for their own liberatory purposes. This insight provides the Invisible College with its revolutionary practice, which is post-Situationist. The Invisible revolutionaries make tactical use of Spectacle and simulation to advance their post-anarchist agenda. This practice corresponds to the post-Situationism of the contemporary radical philosopher Jacques Rancière, who locates the "emancipation" of the spectator in the recognition that "every spectator is already an actor in her story; every actor [...] the spectator of the same story" (Rancière, 2011: 17). Rancière rejects the idea of the "passive" spectator; he views the spectator as an active agent of cultural and political change. Morrison also emphasizes the agency of the spectator. "Embrace the Spectacle," says Morrison. "Learn how to use it" (quoted in Neighly & Cowe-Spigai: 2003: 253).

Hakim Bey's 1987 manifesto "Post-Anarchism Anarchy" included a Baudrillardian call to take up the struggle where the Situationists left off in 1968 (Bey, 2003 [1985]: 62). Bey declared that anarchism "comes closest to our understanding of reality, ontology, the nature of being" (Bey, 2003 [1985]: 62). Post-anarchism contains an ontological anarchy, and it has from the beginning. *The Invisibles* implements this anarchy, as when King Mob decides to reject revolutionary violence and "opt for *ontological* terrorism" (Morrison, 2012: 1198). *The Invisibles'* ontological anarchism manifests most clearly in the comic's rejection of Manichaean dualism. Bey's ontological anarchy proclaims that anarch and king are one and the same (Bey, 2003 [1985]: 66). This becomes the message of *The Invisibles*, particularly in its third and final volume (1999-2000). As Nick James argues, Morrison's ontological terrorism challenges the distinctions between anarchism and authoritarianism to create "a more relevant and less dualistic form of anarchism" (James, 2007: 436): a post-anarchism.

By the late 1990s, Morrison could clearly see the influence of his ground-breaking comic book. On television, the original run of *The X-Files* (1993-2002) drew on the same 1990s conspiracy paranoia that fueled *The Invisibles* (Meaney, 2011: 26). Pop culture was becoming increasingly Invisible. "What you got [then] was that whole thing with *Matrix* culture and the super-heroes coming back – *Buffy*, and the whole thing. And suddenly, there was the fetish gear, the short hair," says Morrison (quoted in Meaney, 2011: 291). In 1999, the Wachowskis (then brothers, later brother and sister, now sisters) released their film *The Matrix*. This film borrowed its theory of simulation, its post-anarchist politics and its fetishistic aesthetic directly from *The Invisibles* (but without crediting Morrison). Joss Whedon's *Buffy the Vampire Slayer* gave television its model of the post-anarchist superhero, especially in season four (1999-2000) (Call, 2011a). But post-anarchism first came to pop culture via the comic book. Grant Morrison brought post-anarchism to comics five years before the Wachowskis brought it to film and Whedon brought it to television. And, *The Invisibles* is not only the birthplace of the post-anarchist superhero. It also provides the origin story for a model of collective action that makes sense in the early years of the third millennium: the *post-anarchist superhero team*.

The Invisibles developed several concepts and critiques that would turn out to be central to the long-term project of post-anarchism. First and foremost, the comic articulated a radical critique of essentialism. This was a harbinger of post-anarchism's major critical trajectory. In 2007, Benjamin Franks identified the "rejection of essentialism" as one of post-anarchism's main emphases (Franks, 2007: 128). By 2016, Saul Newman could point to a "new political subject" whose "ontologically anarchic existence [...] is no longer defined by biological essence, vocation, project or destiny" (Newman, 2016: 37). Twenty years after *The Invisibles* modeled an anti-essentialist political subjectivity within the framework of pop culture, Newman found such a subject in the social world. Life had imitated art – or more precisely, "real world" social movements had evolved along with the pop culture artifacts that represented those movements, to the benefit of both.

The Invisibles also anticipated the rejection of strategic thinking and action that would eventually become a defining feature of post-anarchism (Franks, 2007: 134). Morrison's Invisible revolutionaries consistently favored the tactical over the strategic. *The Invisibles* promoted an ontological anarchy which, as Newman argued in 2016, frees action from "strategic rationality" (Newman, 2016: 10). The tactical model of political action which Grant Morrison's Invisible College utilized throughout the late 1990s eventually became the default model for activism in the social world. This model rejected large-scale strategic actions in favor of provisional, local, tactical interventions. This preference for the tactical over the strategic characterized the wide variety of radical new social movements which Richard J. F. Day described in 2005 (Day, 2005). Day examined the anti-globalisation, environmentalist, and indigenous rights movements, direct action groups such as "Reclaim the Streets" and "Food not Bombs," and radical art groups like "Art and Revolution" and "Bread and Puppets" (Day, 2005: 19-31, 39-41). These groups have shown a particular fondness for Situationist tactics such as zero-work and *détournement* (Day, 2005: 20-3). They have also made effective use of the tactical affinity groups and Temporary Autonomous Zones that Hakim Bey advocated (Day, 2005: 35-6). These groups and their tactics have helped to make post-anarchism something more than an abstract intellectual phenomenon. Twenty years ago, the tactical direct action of Grant Morrison's Invisible College gave late twentieth century post-anarchism a cultural reality; today the tactical actions of the new social movements give early twenty-first century post-anarchism a definite *social* reality.

Clearly, *The Invisibles* can help us understand the post-anarchist tradition of which it is a part, but the reverse is also true: the insights of post-anarchism can help us comprehend the subversive political potential of *The Invisibles*, and of comics in general. Post-anarchism's fascination with the tripartite Lacanian model of reality is especially important here. Prose literature operates within Lacan's Symbolic order; no matter how radical its authors may wish to be, prose language always remains complicit with the Law and with authority. Comics, however, are an image-rich visual medium; as such, they can operate at the level of the Lacanian Imaginary. Imaginary pictures can approach desire and fantasy more closely than Symbolic words can do. Moreover, the Imaginary visuals of comic books reduce the risk that comics will inadvertently reproduce the prohibitions, restrictions and denials that lie at the heart of Symbolic language.

Yet comics participate in the Symbolic too, for they contain words as well as pictures. Comics have traditionally been viewed as a combination of words and images. But Scott McCloud, a respected comic artist and influential comic critic, believes that comics are actually much more than that. In his landmark critical work *Understanding Comics*, McCloud argues that "it's a mistake to see comics as a mere hybrid of the graphic arts and prose fiction" (1993: 92). McCloud views comics as a unique art form which has the power to produce "a kind of magic *only* comics can create" (1993: 92). For McCloud, the power of this "magic" not only exceeds that of prose and graphics considered as individual media; the power of comics is also greater than the sum of their graphic and prose parts. Not only can comics transcend the limits of Symbolic prose and Imaginary visuals; they can even transcend the limits of the prose/graphic combination, to create something truly new.

Tellingly, McCloud emphasizes the unique capabilities of the comics medium by describing comics, in the subtitle of his book, as "the invisible art." McCloud's book was published in 1993, a year before *The Invisibles* began; Morrison's "Invisiblism" bears traces of McCloud's theory of the "invisible art." McCloud argues that comics employ "the whole world of visual iconography [...] and the *invisible* world of symbols and language" (McCloud, 1993: 202-3; emphasis in original). Comics erode the boundaries between visible and invisible (McCloud, 1993: 92), between Symbolic and Imaginary, between writers and artists and readers. Comics permit their readers to partake of a radical new form of subjectivity, one which moves easily between the Symbolic and the Imaginary without becoming trapped in either. While pure prose always runs the risk of degenerating into language's authoritarian, subject-centered form, the ever-present visual aspect of comics effectively mitigates that risk. Comics present the possibility of a libertarian language akin to the "minor languages" of Deleuze and Guattari. The libertarian language of comics can draw upon the power of the image to free the Symbolic from its reactionary commitment to essentialist subjectivities. Read in this light, *The Invisibles* is simply the most explicit example of a post-anarchist possibility that exists throughout the medium of comics.

"When Have I Ever Been Myself, Darling?": Post-anarchist Subjectivity in *The Invisibles*

The Invisibles understands identity in purely post-modern terms. The members of the comic's Invisible cell occupy a broad range of racial, gender, and sexual identities

(Singer, 2012: 107). This fits with Morrison's aggressive post-modern egalitarianism. "I don't give a fuck what gender you are, or whether you're a worm or a zebra," he declares (quoted in Sneddon, 2012: n.p.). More importantly, members of the Invisible cell change identities and take on each other's identities. The provisional nature of identity in *The Invisibles* makes it impossible for any character or group to attain permanent authority. As the Invisible revolutionaries modify, subvert, and trade their identities, they limit and undermine their political authority. Ultimately, these Invisible post-anarchists seek to abolish the individual self altogether and elevate humanity into the egoless world of the Supercontext (Singer, 2012: 131). The Supercontext can be read as a progressive social system based on the free swapping of identities (Meaney, 2011: 208). It is a representation of a post-anarchist society, for as Franks points out, post-anarchism is characterized by an emphasis on "changeable social identities" (2007: 134).

The philosophy of Invisiblism is explicitly designed to overcome individual identity. The Invisible College trains new recruits at the Invisible Academy, where instructor Elfayed teaches this: "Understand. There is *no* 'I am.'" (Morrison, 2012: 723). King Mob models the attainment of this teaching. King Mob is of course not a name but a title. During the Gordon Riots of 1780, the graffito "King Mob" proclaimed the liberation of the inmates of Newgate Prison. In the 1960s, *The King Mob Echo* was a magazine for Situationist pranksters (Meaney, 2011: 314). When the Invisible College's King Mob is captured and tortured by the Outer Church's Sir Miles, he can convincingly claim not to know who King Mob is. "They're some kind of anarchist group from the sixties, aren't they?," says King Mob (Morrison, 2012: 442). So King Mob's "identity" is a radical political practice, and an effective one. He may be a Polish man called Gideon Starorzewski. This name is Anglicized to Gideon Stargrave, who is a character in the comic-within-a-comic that runs throughout *The Invisibles*. Gideon Stargrave was also the title character in an early comic strip that Grant Morrison wrote and drew for *Near Myths* in the late 1970s (Hasted, 1995: 56). Under torture, King Mob claims to be a writer called Kirk Morrison (Morrison, 2012: 441): here the author/character boundary is very thin. King Mob "is" Starorzewski, Stargrave and Morrison in some sense, but since his identity structure features multiple, nested layers of fictionality, he cannot have any fixed or real identity. Thus, King Mob implements the post-anarchist subversion of stable identities.

Lord Fanny models a different kind of subversive identity structure. Fanny was born a boy, and became a girl in order to follow in the footsteps of her female forebears, who had been sorcerers for countless generations (Morrison, 2012: 346-7). This "boygirl" eventually became the powerful shaman Lord Fanny. Fanny's identity is queer (Meaney, 2011: 67, note 15): Morrison's narrative suggests that a person of fixed gender could not have gained the mystic powers that Fanny wields. Only the post-modern androgyny of the boygirl who becomes a sheman could produce that kind of power. Fanny understands the nature of her non-identity: "Myself? When have I ever been myself, darling?" (Morrison, 2012: 336). Fanny's flexible identity

"Lord Fanny (with Mr. Quimper in the wallpaper)."
Art by Brian Bolland.

turns out to be vitally important to the Invisible College's political project. For example, Fanny successfully impersonates her female comrade Ragged Robin, in order to deceive the Outer Church's Mr. Quimper. "Darling … ever get the feeling you've been had?" she purrs to the defeated Quimper (Morrison, 2012: 1134-5). Performance comes easily to the cross-dressing Fanny.

The organizational structure of an Invisibles cell reflects the flexible, fluid identity structure which is such a basic part of both Invisiblism (Meaney, 2011: 116) and post-anarchism. King Mob explains: "Invisibles cells tend to model their structure around elemental symbolism. We each take on a different role within the group. And every so often, we like to change it around and scramble it up a bit. That way everybody gets a chance to assume each of the elemental roles and all the tasks and responsibilities that go with it" (Morrison, 2012: 695). In this way, the Invisible College avoids the dangers of revolutionary vanguardism. This is a particularly post-anarchist aspect of Invisiblism; as Franks notes, post-anarchism typically repudiates vanguard tactics (2007: 128). Invisibles cells have no permanent leaders. When it's time to change roles, cell members gladly hand their role over to one of their comrades and take on a new one. King Mob is happy to give Robin his leadership role. "Well, at least I don't have to be leader anymore," he remarks (Morrison, 2012: 700). Two years later, the cell members switch roles again. "New personalities, new roles. The rules have changed overnight. That's how easy it is to be somebody new," King Mob assures his ally Mason Lang (Morrison, 2012: 1197). Mason is skeptical: "You can just change who you *are* that easily?" King Mob gives a very post-anarchist response: "I can change what I *do* that easily. It's almost the same thing." King Mob has no fixed identity; he is defined by his actions. If he changes his behavior, he changes who he *is*. In this case he throws away his gun (the symbol of violence which has defined him through the first two volumes of the comic) and opts for ontological terrorism (Morrison, 2012: 1198).

As the Invisible revolutionaries approach the Supercontext which marks the culmination of the comic's narrative, they work tirelessly to overcome all ego-based identities. On the eve of the Supercontext, King Mob watches a video broadcast which proclaims that "the very concept of the individual, like that of the bounded nation-state was not designed to survive the last millennium and must be transcended" (Morrison, 2012: 1466). Deleuze and Guattari suggest that the modern nation-state was defined by its boundaries, its territoriality; for them, the nomadic "war machine" exists outside the sovereignty of the state and "prior to its law" (Deleuze & Guattari, 1987: 352). This exteriority recognizes no archon and knows no law: it therefore represents a serious anarchistic threat to the nation-state. Deleuze and Guattari follow Bey in identifying this "outside of States" with "bands, margins, minorities" (Deleuze & Guattari, 1987: 360): Invisibles! By connecting the modern notion of the individual to the idea of the bounded nation-state, Morrison suggests that the former is equally vulnerable to the forces of nomadic anarchy. As the narrative of *The Invisibles* reaches its conclusion, its theory of subjectivity becomes explicitly post-modern. "Multiple personality disorder" becomes "a lifestyle option" (Morrison, 2012: 1466). Indeed, it is the preferred option. Douglas Wolk points out that the most enlightened characters in *The Invisibles* all have multiple personalities

(2007: 267). This corresponds precisely to Deleuze's post-modern concept of subjectivity. "Who speaks and acts?," asks Deleuze. "It is always a multiplicity, even within the person who speaks and acts" (Foucault & Deleuze, 1977: 206). In the post-modern condition, we are all multiple. The Supercontext beckons: the end of Morrison's narrative marks the beginning of a pure anarchy of subjectivity.

The Invisibles also models an anarchy of sexuality that presents consensual dominance/submission (DS) and fetishism as ethical practices. The emphasis on consent means that the sexual politics of Invisiblism are anarchistic. The Marquis de Sade appears in the comic as an eighteenth century member of the Invisible College. Sade summarizes problematic power concisely: "Authority and submission. There's civilization for you" (Morrison, 2012: 196). Sade, of course, is a radical critic of this "civilization," built as it is on authoritarian principles. Transplanted to the late twentieth century, Sade tours a club dedicated to the sexuality that bears his name, S&M (Morrison, 2012: 211). While the Marquis admires this "brave new world," he also recognizes the danger inherent in the exchange of power. "People are afraid to grow up and take responsibility for their lives. They want a mummy, a daddy, a teacher to punish them and tell them where and when to pee" (Morrison, 2012: 211). Here Sade is describing what the Frankfurt School called the authoritarian personality. This mentality is the psychological basis for fascism and other hierarchical political systems. It manifests in the figures of the father, the teacher, the judge and the governess: "Domination. Submission. Britannia in buckled leathers and spiked heels" (Morrison, 2012: 129). This is the oppressive kind of DS: the kind that is woven into the psychological and institutional fabric of society. Sir Miles shares this kind of DS with Miss Dwyer, a demonic representative of the Outer Church. Miles knows what Dwyer is: a "corpse-goddess stinking of death and lust" (Morrison, 2012: 480). Yet he cannot resist her. Miss Dwyer reminds Miles of his place in the hierarchy. "Get down on your knees," she commands, and he obeys instantly (Morrison, 2012: 471). "You're forgetting that little word . . . ," she tells him. He whispers (in small letters) "Mistress." This is fascist, statist submission; Dwyer *is* Britannia in buckled leather, the strict governess enforcing the existing social and political order.

Yet, *The Invisibles* contrasts this reprehensible authoritarian DS with a very different kind, one that is ethical and erotic. The comic is centrally concerned with what the Invisible Mister Six calls "the correct use of power" (Morrison, 2012: 618). Its concerns about power are thus aligned with those of both anarchism and DS. Fetishism signifies power in *The Invisibles*, but the comic makes it clear that this power and the symbols that signify it are available to anyone. Despite his ruthless interrogation techniques, Sir Miles cannot positively identify King Mob, because "any number of men [. . .] involved in the 'fetish' subculture" would match his description (Morrison, 2012: 446). Here power's signifiers are detached from any particular person, and so King Mob can conceal his identity from Sir Miles. The sign of power is arbitrary, and the members of the Invisible cell make effective political use of this structuralist insight. When the cell members trade roles, King Mob gives the signifiers of power to Robin. The change in leadership is signified by a costume change. "Bad

"Robin's fetish gear signifies her new leadership role."
Art by Phil Jimenez and John Stokes.

luck, love," King Mob tells Robin. "You get to wear the leather" (Morrison, 2012: 700). The next panel occupies a full page. Phil Jimenez (probably the best of *The Invisibles* artists) places Robin in the foreground, in a black leather bodysuit, studded leather harness, fishnet stockings, and black boots (Morrison, 2012: 701). Jack stares open-mouthed as this newly minted fetish goddess lays out the plan. "Work it, baby," says Fanny. Robin's leather fetish gear signifies her temporary assumption of the role of team leader. In that role she wields considerable power, but this temporary power was assigned to her by the role-switching lottery, to which all consented. The comic legitimizes Robin's consensual power by eroticizing it. She becomes a Mistress, but unlike Miss Dwyer, her power is ethical.

About halfway through *The Invisibles'* narrative, the Outer Church's Mr. Quimper takes control of Ragged Robin's mind. This plotline gives *The Invisibles* a chance to contrast the Invisible College's consensual DS with the Outer Church's authoritarian dominance. Naked on top of King Mob, Robin wonders if she is the right person to handle the responsibility of being leader. "Sometimes you just want to be told what to do, you know?" (Morrison, 2012: 841). But that is just the Quimper talking. Quimper has become the policeman in Robin's head, the psychological source of her submission to authority. As Quimper's control increases, the nature of his power becomes clear. Robin plays strange games with King Mob in bed. "I've been a rebellious, insubordinate girl: you'd better turn me into a mindless, state-controlled robot before I cause any more trouble" (Morrison, 2012: 1009). This, of course, is precisely what Quimper has done to her. (It's also a parody of what authoritarianism tries to do to everybody.) Robin's comrades will not let Quimper's statist brainwashing stand. Fanny discovers Quimper's presence in Robin's mind and liberates her from his control.

In the end, Robin turns out to be the most powerful Invisible. She is the one who brings on the Supercontext, by traveling through time. Robin returns from her time travels to find King Mob, moments before the advent of the Supercontext. "I'm ready to play with the grown-ups," says King Mob (Morrison, 2012: 1480). His relationship with Robin has allowed him to grow up and take responsibility: he has overcome the authoritarian psychology Sade described previously. Sade could well say of Robin what he says of the twentieth century Invisible revolutionary Helga: "the women of this century embody so many of the strengths I dreamed of" (Morrison, 2012: 1317).

"Welcome to the *Word*:" The Advent of the Post-anarchist Symbolic

The Invisibles' strongest post-anarchist element is its theory of language. Morrison's understanding of language is structuralist. For him, "language makes things slippery. Language is allusive, it changes shape, it can be anything" (quoted in Meaney, 2011: 283). This corresponds to Ferdinand de Saussure's thesis of the arbitrary sign. For Morrison, as for Saussure, there are no necessary connections between signifiers (language that names things) and signifieds (things that language names). In Lacanian terms, *The Invisibles* considers the elusive, mysterious relationship between the

Symbolic, the Imaginary, and the Real. The comic's most radical thought experiments consider the ways in which one of Lacan's orders might overwhelm, supersede, and consume the others. The Outer Church pursues a strategic elimination of the distinction between signifier and signified. They would see the Symbolic collapse through the Imaginary and into the Real. Their ultimate objective is a nightmarish world in which interpretation, language and thought itself are impossible. The Invisible College, on the other hand, collapses signifier and signified tactically and temporarily, to preserve the overall freedom of signification that the arbitrary sign provides. The comic presents the Invisible College's tactical assaults on oppressive forms of symbolic language as viable means for preserving freedom through signification. While Marc Singer argues that the larger project of *The Invisibles* is to transcend symbolic communication entirely (2012: 118), I argue the opposite. The ultimate agenda of Morrison's Invisible revolutionaries is to liberate signification by bringing on the purely Symbolic world of the Supercontext. Ironically, they use the Imaginary and the Real tactically in order to achieve this.

In the realm of the Outer Church, "things are stripped of all meaning, all significance, all association but that which is determined by Control" (Morrison, 2012: 720). Signification is impossible here; signifier and signified are one, and the comic presents this as a profoundly authoritarian environment. Quimper summarizes the reality of the Outer Church: in this place "what is, is. Nothing is open to interpretation" (Morrison, 2012: 1117). In this horrific world, there is only the Real; the Symbolic, which is the realm of interpretation, does not exist. The Outer Church also seeks to eliminate signification in *our* world: "things will be made whole and unambiguous" (Morrison, 2012: 1418). The revolutionaries of the Invisible College will fight to the death to prevent this apocalypse of the Symbolic order.

The Invisible College uses the Imaginary to good effect against the Outer Church, particularly as they work to subvert Quimper's control over Robin's mind. "I want to obey," says Robin, naked beneath King Mob. The image of Quimper looks on from the hotel room's mirror (Morrison, 2012: 1009). This suggests the Lacanian mirror stage, that powerfully Imaginary time when the subject identifies with an image and forms an ego. Here Robin appears to be identifying with the image of the authoritarian Quimper as he becomes her ego. She gazes into the mirror above her make-up table, removes the white "Raggedy Ann" makeup that constitutes her as Ragged Robin, and gazes into the mirror again. The reader sees the reflected image of the "natural" Robin, but she sees Quimper: in the next panel, she puts on a Quimper mask. "Uncanny, darling," says Fanny when she first sees Robin in the mask (Morrison, 2012: 1101). This encourages us to pursue a psychoanalytic reading. Quimper confirms this reading when he reveals that he has been using "the sick, suppressed memory of first betrayal" to control Robin: a memory of incestuous sex with her father (Morrison, 2012: 1131). It seems that Quimper has found a way to keep Robin trapped in this situation forever, and thus ensure that she never hears what Lacan called the Name-of-the-Father, the prohibition of incest. Without that Name, without the repression of incestuous desire, Robin could never enter the Symbolic. But this is where Quimper learns that the mirror image of himself that he has been gazing at is actually not Robin but Lord Fanny. Fanny gives the punch line:

"Robin was never abused by her father. The memory was a fake" (Morrison, 2012: 1140). The mirror works both ways. Quimper has identified with the false Imaginary image of the incestuous Robin. So, in fact it is Quimper who can never leave the Oedipal situation, Quimper who can never leave the mirror stage, Quimper who is denied entry into the Symbolic. Robin and her comrades have won this Imaginary battle.

The shamans of the Invisible College use magical tactics to preserve the Symbolic while disrupting its oppressive aspects. Morrison says that anyone who is interested in language will come to magic eventually (quoted in Gunn, 2014: n.p.). Lord Fanny knows "the secret common language of shamans – that language whose words do not describe things but *are* things" (Morrison, 2012: 399). In this magical language, signifier and signified are one and the same. Hakim Bey calls this language sorcery, "the manipulation of symbols (which are also things)" (Bey, 2003 [1985]: 22). The vocabulary of sorcery is "both real & unreal" (Bey, 2003 [1985]: 22). The sorcerer's language is simultaneously Symbolic, Imaginary and Real, which is why it is so powerful and so dangerous. The Real aspect of such a language might overwhelm its other aspects. Magic could thus inadvertently advance the agenda of the Outer Church. But there is no risk that Fanny's magic will produce a permanent crisis of the Symbolic order. She is too unreal herself, and she signifies too many different things: boygirl, sheman, shaman, Invisible.

Both the Invisible College and the Outer Church use the "Key" drugs, powerful psychedelics that make the user "unable to tell the difference between the word describing an object and the object itself" (Morrison, 2012: 465). These drugs eliminate the distinction between signifier and signified, forcing language to take on an unnatural referentiality. Marc Singer reads the Key drugs as "defiant assertions" of language's referentiality (2012: 120), but I argue that they have the opposite effect. These drugs are the exception that proves the rule. The bizarrely referential language that they create only serves to highlight the *non*-referentiality of ordinary language. To be blunt, it takes hardcore hallucinogens to make signifier equivalent to signified. Sir Miles doses King Mob with Key 17 during his interrogation. Luckily King Mob, like Fanny, is many people signifying many things: Miles can force him into the Real, but he cannot keep him there.

Towards the end of *The Invisibles*' narrative, the Outer Church conspires to bring the King Archon into our world. The King Archon is the deity that the Outer Church worships; it is the apotheosis of authoritarianism. The King Archon is the ultimate monster of the Real; its arrival would spell the disastrous death of the Symbolic. Sir Miles plans to use Jack Frost as the Archon's host body, but Jack's comrade Jolly Roger shoots Miles with Key 23. Miles' temporary exit from the Symbolic order gives Jack the opportunity to consume the Archon (Morrison, 2012: 1446). "I ate him," says Jack. The words seem strangely anticlimactic, but it makes sense that the victory over the Real would be expressed in a simple Symbolic sentence: subject verb object, and the Real returns to the Other Side, where it belongs.

"King Mob defeats the King Archon by shooting a signifier."
Art by Frank Quitely and John Stokes."

As King Mob prepares to enter the Supercontext, he confronts the King Archon one last time. Two Kings face each other; the fate of the Symbolic hangs in the balance. "You were dosed with logoplasm; Key 64, you evil shit," says King Mob (Morrison, 2012: 1476). "Welcome to the *word*. And a bullet in the right place . . . is no substitute for the *real* thing" (Morrison, 2012: 1476-7). King Mob fires his gun, which emits no bullet, but only a red flag with the word "POP" in yellow. King Mob has fired a signifier; Key 64 makes it the Real thing. The Archon vanishes. Morrison narrates the King Archon's defeat in a text box: "[t]he Supercontext absorbs the king effortlessly, welcoming his quaint ferocity, converting it to narrative" (Morrison, 2012: 1477). The Supercontext turns out to be a narrative zone, a Symbolic realm, a world of pure language. Thanks to the anarchy of subjectivity, this Symbolic world can promise liberation: the Supercontext is language uncontaminated by ego. "Who is speaking?" asks Morrison, now at his most Deleuzian. "Whose voice is this speaking in your head and reminding you that freedom is free?" (Morrison, 2012: 1477). The voice is no one's, for the Supercontext is speech without speaker. This speech offers freedom of the post-anarchist sort: freedom from the tyranny of symbol linked to subject. On the last page of *The Invisibles*, Jack quotes Elfayed: "We made gods and jailers because we felt small and ashamed and alone" (Morrison, 2012: 1482). Here at the end, Elfayed and Jack name the traditional enemies of anarchism: religion and the state. They show how those foes have used the Symbolic to oppress us, and they point to a way out: "We let them try us and judge us and, like sheep to slaughter, we allowed ourselves to be . . . sentenced. See! Now! Our sentence is up" (Morrison, 2012: 1482). The series ends with these last four words, big, bold, and black. Then everything fades to white. This is the revenge of the Symbolic: language expands until it encompasses everything. The Symbolic consumes both the Real and the Imaginary (for there is no image in that final white panel). But this is a Symbolic purged of subjectivity and thus liberated from the tyranny of subject-centered language. Like the Invisiblism that spawned it, the Supercontext is a self-realizing discourse, "a thought thinking itself" (Morrison, 2012: 1367).

Marc Singer suggests that "the Invisibles seek to bypass both the tyranny of absolute correspondence and the chaos of floating signifiers by using a language of subjective experience" (2012: 123). He is almost right. The Invisibles certainly resist the Outer Church's attempt to create a permanent equation between signifier and signified. They also reject linguistic chaos. There are no floating signifiers in the Supercontext, for there is no reality above which such signifiers might float. But the Invisibles do not follow the path of the subjective. Their path leads to the dissolution of subjectivity in the rarefied Symbolic realm of the Supercontext. Singer suggests that Jack's final words move from the Symbolic to the Imaginary to the Real in a kind of "Lacanian regression" (Singer, 2012: 126), but I maintain that the ultimate destination of *The Invisibles*' narrative is the Symbolic itself. Douglas Wolk points out that at the end of *The Invisibles*, words replace drawings; in the final panels, Wolk notes, "the sign we see is generated directly by the written representation of language" (2007: 277). The Supercontext is the Symbolic in its most immediate form.

Ragged Robin's writing offers us another example of subjectless language that expands to incorporate everything, including the Real. Robin comes from the future;

in her future world, she drifts in a language-processing "Ganzfeldt Tank," writing a book called *The Invisibles*. As Meaney notes, Robin's experience in the tank represents Morrison's concept of the "fiction suit," a device that allows a writer to enter a fictional universe (Meaney, 2011: 190). Indeed, Morrison says that *The Invisibles* "became the fiction suit concept" (quoted in Meaney, 2011: 302). Morrison used the idea of the fiction suit to enter the narrative as King Mob (also as Jack and Fanny). Robin uses it to write herself into the comic we are reading.

Standing naked in the desert with King Mob, Robin talks about the writing experience. "It turned out there *was* no author. Or maybe the author was *me*" (Morrison, 2012: 1177). The author of *The Invisibles* may be Robin, or Grant Morrison, or no one at all, or the reader of *The Invisibles*. Morrison says that a fangirl sent him the idea: "*what if Ragged Robin wrote the whole thing?*" (quoted in Neighly & Cowe-Spigai, 2003: 252). As Singer notes, *The Invisibles* shifts authorial control from Morrison to the characters and ultimately to the readers (2012: 106). Robin recognizes the danger of the fiction suit: "I'm scared if I write myself in, I'll never get out. They'll find me trapped here in my own words" (Morrison, 2012: 1157). But the fiction suit also offers a more liberatory possibility. It can make fictional language real. "If I write hard enough and honestly enough, I think I can make it real," Robin decides. She understands that a highly concentrated Symbolic narrative can overwhelm the Real to become real itself. When Robin's friend Kerry tells her that she is putting too much symbolism into the story, Robin insists that "it's not symbolism, it's reality" (Morrison, 2012: 1147). Her language has erupted out of the Symbolic order, consuming and replacing the Real.

"It's All Symbolic": Simulation, Spectacle and Symbol in *The Invisibles*

As the narrative of *The Invisibles* unfolds, the Symbolic gradually overtakes and displaces the Real. Thus, the comic's characters enter the realm of simulation. In this realm, the signs of the real are substituted for the real itself (Baudrillard, 1994 [1981]: 2). Language may once have pretended to represent reality. But at the end of the twentieth century, "simulation envelop[ed] the whole edifice of representation itself as a simulacrum" (Baudrillard, 1994 [1981]: 6). Representational language gave way to a language that is its own beginning, ending and referent. This language of simulation dominates the latter part of *The Invisibles'* narrative: it is the liberated language of the Symbolic Supercontext.

The Invisible revolutionaries gradually become aware of the simulated nature of their environment, and they become comfortable in that environment. Gazing at the horrific image of an Archon of the Outer Church, Jack says "it's like something out of a film, like a computer simulation" (Morrison, 2012: 592). Jack begins to understand that he lives in a world where the simulation is real. He turns on the TV: "Is 'Xena' on anywhere? I gotta get a bit of fucking *realism* into my life" (Morrison, 2012: 949). Jack also understands that the level of simulation is increasing over time. "The world gets more like Disneyland every day, and it's the same the other way round" (Morrison, 2012: 1239). Here Jack becomes a mouthpiece for Baudrillard, who saw Disneyland as a perfect model of simulation (Baudrillard, 1994 [1981]: 12). King Mob is a bit more uneasy about simulation. "It's like a stupid film. The whole thing . . . I don't know what's real anymore" (Morrison, 2012: 1064). Robin gives him the hard truth: "maybe *none* of it's real." King Mob shares his concerns with Jack: "what would you do if none of it was *real*, Jack?" (Morrison, 2012: 1091). Jack is delightfully unconcerned. "Don't matter to me. I don't care if it's all one big magic mushroom trip, man. My head's been right around the fucking block. I'm *bigger* than I was" (Morrison, 2012: 1092). Jack has discovered the secret power of simulation. If he embraces simulation rather than fighting it, then his life becomes deeper and richer and more interesting. He can become whatever he wants to be. King Mob finally comes to accept and cherish the reality of simulation. "The world's getting more like *us* every day," he observes. "It's everything I ever hoped for. *Everything* is real" (Morrison, 2012: 1265). King Mob has recognized the power of pure simulation. Once the simulation becomes reality, those who have learned to live in the realm of simulacra can effect real political change there. Thus, Baudrillard argues that "it is in this tactical universe of the simulacrum that one will need to fight" (Baudrillard, 1994 [1981]: 152). This fits with the post-anarchist practice of the Invisible College, which prefers the tactical to the strategic.

Eventually the Invisible revolutionaries learn that they are living "in a world where the symbol [is] more important than the reality" (Morrison, 2012: 1184). Once they understand that the Symbolic has displaced the Real, it does not take them long to realize that they can control the Symbolic. In a world where the symbol is real, the ability to manipulate the symbol is equivalent to the power to change reality. Television may indeed "create the illusion we mistake for reality," but, as King Mob realizes, "those same effective weapons are at our disposal" (Morrison, 2012: 1233). The Invisibles can seize the engines of simulation and use them for revolutionary purposes, e.g. by broadcasting "Invisible TV" (Morrison, 2012: 1217).

Nick James is quite right to suggest that the Invisible College's "anarchist project is the endeavor to dominate the Spectacle" (2007: 447). Mason Lang – perhaps the most media savvy Invisible – says that, "the *image* rules the world. The hallucination has taken control" (Morrison, 2012: 1087). Mason understands that he and his fellow Invisibles live in a world of spectacle and simulation. He also understands that they must develop a political practice suitable for such a world. "How do we take control of the hallucination?" he demands. King Mob's reply explicitly positions the politics of Invisiblism as Situationist: "Mason, you, me and Guy Debord can carry on this conversation some other day" (Morrison, 2012: 1088).

The Invisible College employs Situationist methods throughout the narrative. Jack first learns about Invisiblism by going on a Situationist *dérive* through London: "drifting aimlessly through the city, making it new and strange" (Morrison, 2012: 72). The most important Situationist tactic in *The Invisibles* is *détournement*, the remixing of cultural signs to produce radically different political effects. Interestingly, the Situationist Rene Viénet recommended the *détournement* of comics as a way of

"Brian Bolland's cover for *The Invisibles* volume 2, number 13."

"restoring to comics their content and importance" (Knabb, 2006: 275). While the *détournement* of high art may undermine that art's importance, *détournement* of pop culture artifacts like comics can have the opposite effect. Ironically, *détournement* of *The Invisibles* increases the power of the comic's post-anarchist message. Brian Bolland's cover for *The Invisibles* volume 2, number 13 features word balloons detourned in a blurry, uneven typewriter font, just as they would have been in Paris in the 1960s. King Mob issues Situationist slogans: "Overthrow the Spectacle! Beneath the sidewalk, the beach!" (Morrison, 2012: 961). In this story, a rival Invisibles cell forces King Mob's cell to generate "auto-critique" and detourn their own speech. *Détournement* forces King Mob and his comrades into a brutally honest discursive environment. "My tits sell anarchy," says Ragged Robin (Morrison, 2012: 967). "The most pernicious image of all is the anarchist hero figure," declares King Mob. "A creation of commodity culture, he allows us to buy into an inauthentic simulation of revolutionary praxis" (Morrison, 2012: 967). Fanny's speech is perhaps the most devastating: "the transvestite, far from being a rebellious or transgressive figure, actually serves the status quo by validating stereotypical images of femininity" (Morrison, 2012: 968). This Situationist auto-critique serves an important political purpose. It ensures that the discourse of Invisiblism will not become totalizing or totalitarian. As James notes, Invisible anarchism goes well beyond orthodox anarchism to reject "*all* authority, including the rejection by the anarchist of anarchist ideology itself" (James 2007: 441). This implies, of course, that the Invisible revolutionaries must also reject the authority of Situationism, and indeed they do. The final issue of the comic declares that "the Situationist diagnosis was trapped in the Either/Or Millennium" (Morrison, 2012: 1464). Even a revolutionary praxis as radical as Situationism could not escape from the rigid binary thinking that characterized the twentieth century. The political practice of Invisiblism must therefore become post-Situationist.

The narrative of *The Invisibles* tends towards a radical critique of binary thinking that culminates in an assault on all dualistic philosophies. As Meaney notes, one of the comic's central ideas is "that Manichaean dualism is an illusion" (2011: 13). Jack uses a post-anarchist tactic against dualism: he mocks the Manichaean. Satan appears in the comic as an agent of the Outer Church. When Satan asks if Jack knows what Manichaean means, Jack (who *does* know; Morrison, 2012: 606) replies, "yeah, it's somebody from Manchester" (Morrison, 2012: 1125). Satan asks a question that recurs throughout *The Invisibles*: "which side are you on?" (Morrison, 2012: 1127). Jack's humor renders the very concept of a vast struggle between radically opposed worldviews absurd: "I'm on the side that's got *butter* on it, I am" (Morrison, 2012: 1127). Other enlightened Invisibles share this skepticism about dualistic conflicts between good and evil. Helga interrogates Sir Miles: "The 'Outer Church' you fear and serve and the 'Invisible College' you want to destroy? *Same address*, Sir Miles" (Morrison, 2012: 1375). At the Invisible Academy, Mister Six reveals the great lie behind the Manichaean worldview. "We are not at war. There is no enemy. This is a rescue operation" (Morrison, 2012: 1213). Here the comic presents one of the major insights of post-anarchism: "that there is no central political struggle" (Franks, 2007: 135). The Outer Church seeks the annihilation of opposites, which it hopes to achieve through the manifestation of the King Archon (Morrison, 2012: 1396). But

Invisible revolutionaries like Helga understand that "twenty-first century warfare is about *becoming* the enemy, recognizing no fundamental differences in your ideologies" (Morrison, 2012: 1397). The Invisible revolutionaries seek to merge with their so-called enemies. The Invisible policeman George Harper speaks of "merging opposites; the sun and moon, the good guys and the bad guys. It's all symbolic" (Morrison, 2012: 1402). It is an apt choice of words. The ultimate destination of *The Invisibles'* narrative is a Symbolic realm where language loses its dualisms, a place without I/you, us/them, good/evil, anarchy/authority. This place is the Supercontext. "Up for a spot of ontological terror?," the man formerly known as King Mob asks Helga in the comic's penultimate issue. "The name's *Gideon*, by the way" (Morrison, 2012: 1457). Gideon has abandoned the name King Mob. He will not need this subjectivity, or any other, when he enters the Supercontext.

Since its inception, post-anarchism has challenged the "binary, Manichaean opposition" between society and the state which Newman views as characteristic of nineteenth century revolutionary anarchism (Newman, 2001: 36) (and which I view as characterizing *some* anarchisms of that period). *The Invisibles* embodies this post-anarchist challenge to Manichaeanism by first presenting a classic struggle between authoritarians and left-libertarians – and then slowly, steadily subverting that struggle. Grant Morrison represents this subversion through the Supercontext, a post-binary environment which dissolves all dialectical dualisms. The Supercontext also represents the victory of a very specific sort of Symbolic, one which has been purged of egoism, essentialism, and the languages which underwrite such subjectivities. The Supercontext thus offers a possible escape from what Fredric Jameson famously called "the prison-house of language" (Jameson 1972). By the time Morrison's Invisible revolutionaries enter the Supercontext, they have learned the major lessons of post-anarchism. They understand that Symbolic language can be a powerful authoritarian force. But they also understand that they can counter language's authoritarian tendencies by leaving their egos behind and embracing the dissolution of their selves. Thus, they discover the irony that lies at the heart of post-anarchism: the post-modern proliferation of multiple intersecting identities means that an effective libertarian philosophy begins, ironically, where unitary individual subjectivity ends.

As they take advantage of this irony, Morrison's Invisible revolutionaries develop and deploy a very post-anarchist political practice. Like the post-anarchist activists whom they represent and inspire, Morrison's Invisibles consistently reject revolutionary vanguardism and large-scale strategic action in favor of small-scale, localized, tactical practices. By rejecting the strategic and embracing the tactical, Morrison aligns his work with that of post-structuralist political activists. Foucault and Deleuze, for example, advocated "localized counter-responses, skirmishes, active and occasionally preventive defenses," arguing that such tactics could effectively challenge centralized, hierarchical power without reproducing such power's forms (1977: 212). The emphasis on the tactical also aligns *The Invisibles* with the post-anarchist heirs of post-structuralism in the new social movements. *The Invisibles* thus provides both a sophisticated post-anarchist theory and a theoretically informed tactical practice. At the tail end of the twentieth century, Grant Morrison's

Invisible College offered a post-anarchist political philosophy which would allow revolutionaries to understand the social and political conditions of the early twenty-first century, and a set of radical tactical practices which they could use to change those conditions. *The Invisibles* occupies a pivotal place in the history of post-anarchism: after the early theoretical experiments of Hakim Bey, before the emergence of a viable post-anarchist political practice in the early years of the third millennium. *The Invisibles* is thus an important bridge between the theory of post-anarchism and its practice.

References

Baudrillard, Jean. (1994) [1981] *Simulacra and Simulation*. (Sheila Faria Glaser, Trans.). Ann Arbor: University of Michigan Press.

Bey, Hakim. (2003) [1985] *T.A.Z.: The Temporary Autonomous Zone, Ontological Anarchy, Poetic Terrorism* (Second Edition). New York: Autonomedia.

Call, Lewis. (2008) "A is for Anarchy, V is for Vendetta: Images of Guy Fawkes and the Creation of Postmodern Anarchism." *Anarchist Studies*, Vol. 16, No. 2: pp. 154-72.

Call, Lewis. (2011a) "Buffy the Post-Anarchist Vampire Slayer," in *Post-Anarchism: A Reader* (Duane Rousselle & Süreyyya Evren, Eds.). London: Pluto Press.

Call, Lewis. (2011b) "Structures of Desire: Postanarchist Kink in the Speculative Fiction of Octavia Butler and Samuel Delany," in *Anarchism & Sexuality: Ethics, Relationships and Power* (Jamie Heckert & Richard Cleminson, Eds.). New York: Routledge.

Day, Richard J. F. (2005) *Gramsci is Dead: Anarchist Currents in the Newest Social Movements*. London: Pluto Press.

Deleuze, Gilles & Félix Guattari. (1987) *A Thousand Plateaus: Capitalism and Schizophrenia* (Brian Massumi, Trans.). Minneapolis: University of Minnesota Press.

Edwards, Gavin. (2012) "The Super Psyche." *Playboy* (May): pp. 76-9.

Foucault, Michel & Gilles Deleuze. (1977) "Intellectuals and Power: a conversation between Michel Foucault and Gilles Deleuze," in Michel Foucault, *Language, Counter-Memory, Practice: Selected Essays and Interviews* (Donald F. Bouchard, Ed.). Ithaca: Cornell University Press.

Franks, Benjamin. (2007) "Postanarchism: A Critical Assessment." *Journal of Political Ideologies*, Vol. 12, No. 2 (June): pp. 127-45.

Gunn, James. (2014) "Grant Morrison." *Interview*. (October 14). As retrieved on April 4, 2018 from <http://www.interviewmagazine.com>

Hasted, Nick. (1995) "Grant Morrison Interview." *The Comics Journal*, No. 176 (April): pp. 52-82.

Hiatt, Brian. (2011) "Grant Morrison: Psychedelic Superhero." *Rolling Stone* (August 22).

James, Nick. (2007) "Opting for Ontological Terrorism: Freedom and Control in Grant Morrison's *The Invisibles*," *Law, Culture and the Humanities*, Vol. 3, No. 3 (October): pp. 435-454.

Jameson, Fredric. (1972) *The Prison-House of Language: A Critical Account of Structuralism and Russian Formalism*. Princeton: Princeton University Press.

Knabb, Ken, Ed., Trans. (2006) *Situationist International Anthology* (Revised Edition). Berkeley: Bureau of Public Secrets.

Lacan, Jacques. (2006) *Écrits: The First Complete Edition in English* (Bruce Fink, Trans.). New York: W. W. Norton.

Marini, Marcelle. (1992) *Jacques Lacan: The French Context* (Anne Tomiche, Trans.). New Brunswick: Rutgers University Press.

May, Todd. (1994) *The Political Philosophy of Poststructuralist Anarchism.* University Park: Pennsylvania State University Press.

McCloud, Scott. (1993) *Understanding Comics: The Invisible Art.* New York: HarperCollins.

Meaney, Patrick, Dir. (2010) *Grant Morrison: Talking with Gods.* Respect Films.

Meaney, Patrick. (2011) *Our Sentence Is Up: Seeing Grant Morrison's* The Invisibles. Edwardsville, Illinois: Sequart Research & Literacy Organization.

Morrison, Grant. (2012) *The Invisibles Omnibus.* New York: DC Comics.

Neighly, Patrick & Kereth Cowe-Spigai. (2003) *Anarchy for the Masses: The Disinformation Guide to The Invisibles.* New York: The Disinformation Company.

Newman, Saul. (2001) *From Bakunin to Lacan: Anti-Authoritarianism and the Dislocation of Power.* Lanham, Maryland: Lexington Books.

Newman, Saul. (2016) *Postanarchism.* Cambridge, UK: Polity Press.

Rancière, Jacques. (2011) *The Emancipated Spectator.* New York: Verso.

Singer, Marc. (2012) *Grant Morrison: Combining the Worlds of Contemporary Comics.* Jackson: University Press of Mississippi.

Sneddon, Laura. (2012) "Grant Morrison: Why I'm Stepping Away from Superheroes," *New Statesman,* Vol. 15 (September). As retrieved on April 4, 2018 from <https://www.newstatesman.com/>

Weiss, Margot D. (2006) "Mainstreaming Kink: The Politics of BDSM Representation in U.S. Popular Media," in *Sadomasochism: Powerful Pleasures* (Peggy J. Kleinplatz & Charles Moser, Eds.). Binghamton, New York: The Haworth Press.

Wolk, Douglas. (2007) *Reading Comics: How Graphic Novels Work and What They Mean.* Philadelphia: Da Capo Press.

5.

The Affective Bases of Domination:
Beyond Marxism and Psychoanalysis

By Christopher*
Translated by Jesse Cohn**

Some have attempted to address the popular acceptance of irrational ideas like fascism or capitalism through various combinations of the work of Marx and different forms of psychoanalysis. Some of the better-known attempts in this regard are Erich Fromm's humanistic psychoanalysis, Wilhelm Reich's discussion of the role of repressed sexuality as a control mechanism, and today, the philosopher Slavoj Žižek's explanation via Marx's theory of commodity fetishism and Lacan's psychoanalysis.

Reich's work can be considered an inadequate tool for understanding the current reality, since, although the restriction of sexuality once played an important role as a system of social control, we now witness the opposite phenomenon: its commercialization.

We can see an advance in Fromm's incorporation of an interactive conjunction between ideology, concrete socioeconomic conditions, and individual psychology, forming a cultural psychoanalysis; however, in an attempt to leave behind Freud's biologism, he neglects the biological and affective dimension that Reich had already pointed out, abstracting it into two forces, one oriented toward life (biophilia) and the other toward death (necrophilia).

Žižek partially takes over the objections made to Fromm and Reich, incorporating a Lacanian psychoanalysis that is quite different from the versions of psychoanalysis cited above, but he falls back into the same dilemma concerning the need for domination and submission which appears in Fromm's work. Žižek represents it as a conflict between accepting our vulnerable condition as living beings or turning it into an all-powerful guarantor of a supposedly absolute and true morality. For this author, capitalism by means of commodity fetishism breaks up all human relationships, turning them into economic relations, with nationalism surviving as a pathological form that attempts to substitute itself for the exposure to this cultural vacuum, forcibly re-creating a myth of community.

---

* Christopher studied psychology at the Universidad de Concepción in Chile. His blog, El virus de la subversión is now defunct. Some have described him as "[i]nterested in a critical science that contributes to the abolition of all forms of domination." Some of his more recent writings under the name "de_humanizer" can be found at the following blog: <http://rebeldealegre.blogspot.cl/>

** Jesse Cohn is the author of *Underground Passages: Anarchist Resistance Culture, 1848-2011* (AK Press, 2015). He translates and teaches English in northwest Indiana.

"Late" capitalism introduces a modification, avoiding identification with an omnipotent leader in favor of an anonymous and apparently neutral techno-science in which is exacerbated the transgression of what was previously forbidden (sexuality, lifestyles prior sanctioned, etc), producing a biopolitics which administers individuals' desires, but which also strips them of their initiative, turning them into passive subjects who give themselves over to the administration of this anonymous techno-science. An idea quite similar to Guy Debord's notion of the diversification of the image of the leader into a panoply of commodities, supposedly able to satisfy every illusion possible, which he describes as the passage from a *concentrated* to a *diffuse* spectacle.

Thus, Žižek points out that the discourse of egalitarianism that capitalism presents, through formal democracy, is a form of totalitarianism to which both the individual and the universal succumb, as the ties that bind us are broken and the aspects that differentiate us disappear, to which Žižek opposes a vision in which the universal is the pursuit of what we have in common starting from what makes us unique.

Žižek's understanding of the current situation seems to me adequate in the sense that, while he repeats the dilemma raised by Fromm, he makes a sharp critique of the idea of egalitarianism; however, in using a Lacanian psychoanalysis focused exclusively on language and the symbolic, Žižek reproduces the same mutilation of the human being we find in postmodernism, this conversion of human beings into a symbolic artifact ramified into a series of ideas, which, in my opinion, serves to limit the chances for a complete emancipation of human beings, since the unit of analysis is an abstraction.

The obvious question is: what is being mutilated? And the answer, as Reich anticipated, is our body and affectivity, the concrete terrain on which biopolitics is administered; however, the restriction of sexuality is not a primary mechanism of coercion right now. This inconsistency is resolved at the level of the most concrete, the affects, which are a psycho-physiological phenomenon at the root of all forms of social relations, from the restriction of sexuality to the fetishism of commodities.

This detail is what allows us to think of a more radical transformation than Žižek can imagine in his most humanitarian visions of a possible administrative system. Let me explain. In the work of Žižek, the central image of psychoanalysis persists: a human being fractured between unconscious and irrational desires that must be harmonized with an external reality. In the case of Lacanian psychoanalysis, this fragmentation operates at a "real," "symbolic," and "imaginary" level, where these three categories are all combined in an interdependent way like three linked rings (the Borromean knot).

These units of analysis, based on the symbolic and on the unconscious and conscious, can be considered fictitious, basically because contemporary neuroscience has discovered that there is nothing like a separation between mind and body, our body being that which by acting mobilizes decentralized groups of neurons, from which emerges a phenomenon that is our mind.

The neurobiologist Francisco Varela describes it by comparing it to a nation which only exists as a phenomenon when its members interact, while the concept of nation cannot be located anywhere when it lacks a concrete embodiment. In this way, our brain and body function like a symphony in which each instrument harmonizes with the others.

This unity of mind and body achieves continuity in action, according to scientific research, but varies constantly in terms of its content, breaking neural connections at one moment and switching to others, as if the melody of the symphony were to change every second. All this continuous movement gives us a sense of identity; if not for this movement, we would be as completely rigid as corpses.

When we are reproduced by a culture, whether based on the coercion or the administration of desires, what we incorporate, not "mentally" but in our actions, is a script or repertoire of limited behaviors which "stiffen" us – that which has wrongly been called "alienation," because it is simply a behavioral, affective, and perceptual pattern, but one of which the particularity is not to produce a sense of "self-estrangement," but which limits our intrinsic capacity for spontaneity.

Taking quantum physics as a model, Žižek thinks that these symbolic levels of Lacan aim to protect us from the total void, so that love or cultural constructs emerge from this general homogeneity as "anomalies" shielding us from these "unconscious" fears. In reality, making a theoretical cut in this void is like trying to understand the idea of a symphony by freezing it and examining how the instruments work one by one, as if *that* were the fundamental reality. In contrast to physics, which goes from an inert universe to a living universe, Varela's neurobiology considers the phenomenon of life to be a movement intrinsic to the universe itself.

This difference in understanding the mind as an emergent property of our concrete activities from an affective tonality, giving a motivational framework to our thoughts, in contrast to the idea of a mind fragmented into a maze of levels from which certain symbols must be extracted from the outside in order to reach an agreement on them with others, produces different results at the moment when reality is transformed, because if we have a human being split [*conflictuado*] between rationality and irrationality or between the conscious and unconscious, the chances for comprehensive emancipation are quite modest.

However, if we rely on experimental evidence, we find a mind-body unity which can be modified at the level of its deepest affects if its own action is altered, while it breaks with this fragmented view of the human being present in psychoanalysis, and we recover a human being which is neither internally nor externally conflicted, since it can peacefully direct its attention to its affects and the ideas that emerge from them.

A human being capable of using its senses in the immediate present demolishes symbolic constructs, thinking from an affective rationality, this phenomenon of being located in the concrete present, totally emptied of previous concepts, in order to perceive and feel a phenomenon, regains its spontaneity and critical reasoning; it is the human being which perceives all ideological controls as a fiction, and which, therefore, is able to recognize its own individuality and that of others, becoming conscious of their interdependence through empathy.

The experience of mind as a fragmented phenomenon distinct from the body, as described in one way or another by all of the psychoanalysts, is not our natural condition, but the effect of cultural programming, at the origin of which is an attempt to resolve the very condition of helplessness of the human being in the face of its own finitude within an environment that is always difficult to predict. There are no contradictions between conscious and unconscious phenomena; rather, we have a faster or slower attention to respond to the affects that disturb us at every moment, and every ideology forcibly focuses on certain aspects, intended to limit a perception and an action other than what is imposed, so that the sensation of conflict is a need for sensory-perceptual decentering, which allows us do something different, a capacity which, over time, can atrophy almost completely until submission is attained, annihilating the critical capacity.

The possibility of change is rooted in the fact that from every human individual, community, etc, a phenomenon emerges in the form of a system which is the product of its concrete social relationships and affective basis; thus, affirming other kinds of social relations based on mutual aid alters this emergent system, and this alteration of the system in turn alters other components of the system in this direction. This change begins when we change our action, which produces an affective restructuring enabling the affirmation of a communist or anarchic society. This provides the affective basis that makes it unnecessary to adhere to hierarchy or hegemonic ideology, because it resolves our condition of helplessness, affirming an interdependent individuality that recognizes both what makes us each singular and what we have in common with others.

In this way, rather than face the false dualisms of the rational versus the irrational, the conscious versus the unconscious, the symbolic versus the concrete, we restructure our affectivity, through forms of dynamic attention that allow us to look and act both inwardly and outwardly at will. From this flexibility in acting, thinking, and feeling there emerges a different human being, because it changes what we are structurally by beginning to change things concretely. This points to the need for a libertarian pedagogy incorporating this emotional education – clearly not in the form of corny self-help books, but as an education in thinking by using our senses, emptying ourselves of preconceived notions when confronting a phenomenon, thinking through each situation in the present moment, i.e., using our faculties in sync with our own biology. A failure to do so lies at the root of any system of domination.

Again, it is important to note that what we intend to describe here, from a libertarian standpoint, is a way to produce an autonomous cultural and material basis from which to oppose the system of domination, which, on reaching a critical mass, breaks the consensus of the dominant ideology, but which in no way excludes violent confrontation, since obviously the ruling class will not voluntarily relinquish its privileges. However, it may contribute to affirming a different world from the innermost depths of individuals, while reducing violence, as a means to an end, as much as possible.

See: https://tinyurl.com/ya4nkppo

Bibliography

Žižek, S. (2002). *For they know not what they do: Enjoyment as a political factor.* London: Verso.

Fromm, E. (2013). *The anatomy of human destructiveness.* New York, N.Y: Open Road Media.

Reich, W. (2000). *The Mass Psychology of Fascism.* New York: Farrar, Straus and Giroux.

Varela, F. J., Thompson, E., & Rosch, E. (2011). *The Embodied Mind: Cognitive Science and Human Experience.* Cambridge, Mass: MIT Press.

6.

Proudhon, Lacan, and the Quilting Points

Daniel Colson*
Jesse Cohn (Intro., Trans.)**

Introduction: A Proudhonian Perspective

Pierre-Joseph Proudhon, a key source of inspiration for Daniel Colson's post-anarchist philosophy, is scarcely remembered at all by Anglo-American readers of theory. When he is remembered, it is generally as the whipping boy for Marx, who dedicated an entire book, *The Poverty of Philosophy* ([1847] 1995), to trashing Proudhon's *Philosophy of Poverty* ([1846] 2011). Caricatured there as a petit-bourgeois moralist dabbling in a Hegelianism he scarcely understands, Proudhon has languished in obscurity ever since, the majority of his works remaining untranslated into English. His reputation – perversely, for someone who famously answered the question "What is property?" with the resounding declaration that "Property is theft!" – is that of a kind of fetishist of the independent small proprietor, a devotee of the untrammeled "liberty" of "the individual." As if this weren't enough, he suffers from the charge leveled at all of the so-called "classical anarchists": pinning his social hopes on a spurious "human nature" that is ostensibly rational, good, gregarious, etc. (see, for example, Koch, 1993). In short, Proudhon appears to us as a musty curiosity from the cabinet of gaudy nineteenth-century utopian doctrines – anything but relevant to a postmodern era.

What Daniel Colson has revealed, in his re-readings of Proudhon, is something entirely different. Contrary to what has been asserted, Proudhon in fact launches a pluralistic assault on all the utopias that aim to reduce human diversity to a single normative image, an inevitably despotic "absolute" (Proudhon [1858] 1935, 3.172). Colson's Proudhon is not a moralist in the sense indicted by Marx or Nietzsche, believing in a self-contained subject who freely subjects himself to a Law that precedes and governs life; he is a kind of pragmatist for whom knowledge is never to be seen as separate from power, for whom signification and force are the two irreducible faces of a single reality. His ethics consist of a continual attempt to negotiate relations of power within the networks of association that constitute not a Rousseauvian "social contract" among independent persons but "collective beings" increasingly capable of expressing all the powers and possibilities they contain.

* Daniel Colson, active in the anarchist movement since the 1960s, is a sociologist and professor at the Université de Saint-Étienne in Lyon. The author of numerous works, including the *Petit lexique philosophique de l'anarchisme de Proudhon à Deleuze* (2001), soon to appear in translation as *A Short Philosophical Dictionary of Anarchism: From Proudhon to Deleuze*, and most recently, *Proudhon et l'anarchie* (2017), he has written extensively for the journals *IRL* (Informations Rassemblées à Lyon / Informations et Réflexions Libertaires) and *Réfractions*, and is a longtime member of the La Gryffe bookstore collective.

** Jesse Cohn is the author of *Underground Passages: Anarchist Resistance Culture*, 1848-2011 (AK Press, 2015). He translates and teaches English in northwest Indiana.

Rather than erecting utopian sandcastles on *a priori*, essentialist foundations, Proudhon is an ontologist of "resultants": all the faculties of what is called "Man" are, like everything else in the universe, "the resultant of a compound of other powers, themselves resulting from other compositions, other forces, etc." (Colson, 2001: 273-4). Every time forces join, the "resultant" is not, as Thomas Hobbes would have it, a mathematical sum, but something qualitatively different, a "collective force" which is both "the expression of the forces and powers which, in composing it, make it possible" and "at the same time more and other, distinct from the forces which render them possible [...] a radically new, autonomous reality" (Colson, 2007: 97-8). In short, the Proudhon who emerges from Colson's interpretation stands in a relation of profoundly mutual illumination with the poststructuralism of Gilles Deleuze.

In this light, it is intriguing to ask what kinds of association Proudhon might enter into with Jacques Lacan. On the one hand, as a Deleuzean, Colson is fiercely opposed to Lacan's psychoanalytic pretensions, and especially to the concept of desire as presupposing lack – a lack that quickly becomes a new (and dismal) foundation for social relations:

> The identification of desire with lack, absence, and deprivation, from Christianity to psychoanalysis, has played an essential role in the subjection of beings to an oppressive order that has become distorted in its power. In place of a conception based on the negative, in which desire, inevitably placed under the sign of *ressentiment*, exists only through the absence of its object, through a castration in which every force is separated from its own capacities, libertarian thought substitutes an identification of desire with power, plenitude, superabundance, and generosity. [...] Whereas, in the theory of desire as lack, the encounter with the other becomes impossible, the libertarian conception of desire and its power continuously make possible an encounter with the totality of other collective forces, on a certain plane of reality, since these forces are also subjective beings, each of which one potentially contains within oneself [...] Every encounter and every difference, however little they avoid the traps (dialectical or otherwise) that external collisions and confrontations never fail to cause, may then serve as the occasion for each to reveal the infinite power that it contains, the occasion for it to exceed its own limits and to do all that it is capable of (Colson, 2005: 180-1; see also Robinson, 2005).

It is for this reason that Colson's fellow Deleuzean, Todd May, has also concluded that Lacanian theory provides "a weak basis for political thought and organizing," as it "tends to drive people apart rather than bringing them together" (2002: 11).

It is perhaps fitting, then, that Colson takes as his point of departure for an exploration of the relationship between Proudhon and Lacan the notion of the "quilting point" or *point de capiton*, this mysterious locus in which incommensurable things are made to converge. Are we watching a rapprochement between philosophical enemies? Or, on the contrary, is Colson practicing that very Deleuzian mode of critique-by-satire, the "buggery" that consists of "taking an author from *behind*, and giving him a *child* that would be his own offspring, yet monstrous" (1995: 6)?

It may be argued that the offspring in question (and, indeed, Deleuze's masculinist metaphor) is illegitimate. Other post-anarchist readings of Lacan, notably Saul Newman's, have construed him as anything but "a structuralist of strict observance," as Colson would have it here. It is possible to emphasize instead the degree to which Lacan departed from structuralism, producing an image of the subject that is discontinuous, unstable, fluctuating, and so on. Nonetheless, Colson draws on rather orthodox primary and secondary sources, and his treatment of Lacan's conception of time – a conception he sees as deeply indebted to the structuralist legacy – is not far from some other contemporary readings, such as Adrian Johnston's, which draw on some of the same passages in Lacan's *Seminars* (See Johnston, 2005: 46-7).

Ironically, Proudhon happens to be one of the only anarchist authors in whom Lacan ever expressed an interest. "I highly recommend you read Proudhon," he remarks in one of his *Seminars*: "he had a solid mind [...] Proudhon, whose every thought runs counter to romantic illusions" (Lacan, 1978: 260). Elsewhere, he puckishly appropriates Proudhon's admonition that "property is theft" (Lacan, 1997: 82). Is it unthinkable that Lacan could be made to bear the impossible offspring of this impossible man?

Jesse Cohn
Purdue University Northwest

Proudhon, Lacan, and the Quilting Points

Daniel Colson

Among the many contradictions that Proudhon refuses to resolve, that he considers essential to life, is one that touches on his own existence.

—On the one hand, repeated endlessly, we find an ontology of becomings and transformations, in which every individual, like everything else, is a "group," necessarily provisional and often evanescent, in a constant state of metamorphosis, a "composite of powers" and "spontaneities," at once a "resultant" and a "component" of a multitude of other entities likewise composed and individuated; actual and virtual entities, included within one another and doubly infinite in number, from the largest to the smallest.

—On the other hand, there is the obstinacy and stubborn self-assertion of the individual named Proudhon, refusing any compromise, any loss or weakening of himself, whether in the indeterminacy of his attitudes or in unspoken, vague, and tentative reconciliations. The individual Proudhon always aims at an absolute mastery of his life, often at the real risk of placing himself in opposition to everyone, of isolating himself and, above all, of endlessly expounding on all subjects, multiplying texts and speeches, seeking to voice, to understand, and to encompass the world, to grasp everything, again from the largest subjects to the smallest and most immediate: socialism, property, federalism, revolution, art, war, peace, order in humanity, anarchy, but also taxes, stock exchange speculation, the railroads, the benefits of chastity, advice to princes and industrialists, the "perpetual exposition," woman's sexual weakness, or personal reflections *ad infinitum* on the reasons for accepting or refusing a duel, marrying or not marrying, etc. Minor or major, written for personal reasons or on request, public or intimate, the topics covered by Proudhon never fail to give rise to endless treatises in which Proudhon the individual tries to say everything and consider everything, without leaving anything out, at the risk of ruining his health and ending up dying at the age of fifty-six. He leaves behind the mass of some incredible twenty thousand printed pages of texts and treaties, stacked, composite, in all their diversity, their eclecticism, their relentless repetition of the different and the variation of their perspectives. In their very heterogeneity, they are homologous to the anarchy of beings that Proudhon the individual is always attempting to think through the various experiences of the libertarian movement once again, through a new object, a new problem, a new pretext, a new perspective, but each time with as much conviction, or, more precisely, "resolution" – an important concept for understanding Proudhon, but also, as we shall see later, for understanding how the improbable Jacques Lacan comes, in his turn, to cross paths with anarchism:

What is it, indeed, that we call a person? And what does this person mean when he says: *Me?* – is it his arm, his head, his body, or his passion, his intelligence, his talent, his memory, his virtue, his conscience? Is it any of his faculties? Is it even the series or synthesis of his faculties, physical and mental? It is all of this, to begin with [...], and more than this. It is his intimate, invisible essence, which conceives itself as a superior existence, sovereign in its liberty, dominating its faculties from on high, disposing of them arbitrarily; [...] in short, an absolute, and an absolute that is not only posited, but an absolute that feels, sees, wants, acts, and speaks (Proudhon, [1858] 1935: 3.172-3).

At once a resultant and an absolute affirmation (*"sui generis"*), each individual is a radically new and autonomous reality which nonetheless depends entirely on the forces that compose it. For Proudhon cannot get around this double statement, an intentional antinomy: the total autonomy of beings and their just as total dependence on the forces that give them a soul and a body (for a time) during brief equilibriums that never stop transforming them and allowing them to say, each from its own side, once more, in a different voice every time: "me," "I want," "I do," "I feel," "I think."

—Hence the succession, in Proudhon, of so-called "stances," with their profound discursive effects, like swollen rivers that swell and overflow of their own accord, and with no shortage of metamorphoses over the course of so many pages, dividing into small rivers and streams, which are themselves, behind the unitary appearance of their turbulent becoming, composed from a multitude of other beings, other forces in a state of becoming, disparate, contradictory, constantly colliding with one another in their swirling evanescence, all aspiring to constitute stances in their turn, wanting to impose their "yoke" upon everything, as Gabriel Tarde says (1999: 57; 2011: 27).

—But this is also the source of Proudhon's anguish, at every moment, in the face of "decisions," from the most ordinary to those taken in the heat of the most terrible events of 1848, for example, when Proudhon once again decided to radically alter his views on the world and the revolution, all the while giving expression to the anguish of this transformation, to the best of his ability, through a new text – a retrospective look at an interval in which, even as we change, we never cease to be the same:

A republican of the college, the workshop, the office, I shivered in terror at what I saw approaching the Republic [...] the social revolution had arisen without anyone, neither from above nor below, seeming to have the intelligence of it. Now what would the revolution do, what would it become, without anyone possessing its secret, its idea! [...] The Revolution, Republic, Socialism, overlapping one another, coming fast! [...] This revolution that was going to burst upon the public order was the zero hour of a social revolution for which nobody had the word. [...]. Thus, everything seemed to me to be alarming, amazing, paradoxical [...] In this devouring anxiety, I rebelled against the drift of events, I dared to condemn destiny. [...] My soul was in agony [...]. On February 21st, in the evening, I still exhorted my friends not to fight. On the 22nd, I breathed when I heard of the opposition backing down; I believed myself at the end of my martyrdom. Then the day of the 23rd came to dissipate my illusions. But this time the die was cast, *jacta est alea*, as M. de Lamartine says. The shooting in the Rue des Capucines changed my dispositions in an instant. I was no longer the same man (Proudhon, 1983: 75).

"I was no longer the same man," writes Proudhon, which means that after a period of anxiety in which he had been lost, Proudhon, in "chang[ing] [his] dispositions," returns to himself in a kind of swooning, becoming the individual Proudhon all over again, the same person and yet another person, still *determined* to see clearly, to grasp everything and understand everything, to write new treatises from new perspectives. This necessary (and intimate) antinomy between the same and the different, between absolute freedom and a no less absolute necessity that gives it its strength and its "resolution" – ("I had to do it!" "I couldn't have done otherwise!") – is not unique to the life and thought of Proudhon. We find it in Déjacque, Coeuderoy, or Bakunin, but also in most of the collective experiences of working-class anarchism. It is found for example in Brazil where, as Jacy de Seixas Alves shows us, the different labor movements of Rio de Janeiro and São Paulo, can, like Proudhon fifty years earlier, display an "insistent and disconcerting unity" even if they are almost unbelievably discontinuous and heterogeneous in their acronyms and organizations, journals, projects, and political and philosophical references, in the nature of the working-class forces they set in motion.[59] It is also found in the "unparalleled plasticity" of direct action described by Pouget, one of the leaders of the French CGT before 1914, direct action having "no specific form" but rather an excess of possible forms, an excess that thus imparts all the power of that which exists to every act, every assertion, every situation, every individual crystallization (Pouget, 2003: 23, 13).

---

[59] On this contrast between unity and disparity, see Seixas (1989).

How to think this extreme tension between the "determinate" and an excessive indeterminacy that gives it its strength and intensity, where the "determinate" and "determination" change meaning, and – due to objective but merely apparent and illusory external constraints – become internal needs? How to think the relationship between the "resolute," this tension between will and "resolution," this way the real anarchy is bound and loosed in constant singular beings acting and thinking, the objective nature obvious even they derive their strength and existence of themselves and their subjective power?[60] From Leibniz's "monads" and the Simondonian account of "individuation," Spinoza's "modes," Nietzsche's "will to power," and Proudhon's "collective beings" to Whitehead's "prehensions," "concrescences," and other "actual entities," we have (also) a great number of concepts with which to address these questions, not in the manner of a multitude of doors opening indifferently, so that "too many taxes kill taxes," as the imbeciles say,[61] but rather to think and then complicate the infinite – in the manner of Proudhon's work, or of children who shout "more!" – starting from the repetition of another infinity of experiences, perceptions, and points of view. The anarchy of that which exists, this "much stranger unity that applies only to the multiple" referred to by Deleuze (Deleuze & Guattari, [1980] 2004: 175), is of course matched by an overabundance of concepts and thus of possible points of view, ways of adapting to [*plier*] and understanding [*appréhender*] the world, from the best known to the most improbable – the Lacanian concept of the "quilting point," for example.

As we know, quilting points are the attachments stitching a surface, such as leather, to the fabric of the upholstery, e.g., on an English armchair or on the old-fashioned doors of a notary's office. Lacan's (original) use of this concept is very interesting in terms of its effects, but we must recognize that it first takes shape in questions as far removed from any anarchist perspective as [Ferdinand de] Saussure's theory of language, in particular the distinction between signifier and signified. As we all know, in Saussurean thought, the signifier is the material and objective aspect of language, with its phonemes, words, and phrases, its internal structure that allows us to distinguish and thus to form signs, while the signified is the idea or concept that these words and phrases are supposed to say and express. The problem for Lacan is: how are the signifier and signified connected to one another? How can the signifier and signified form blocs of meaning, beings, or entities that make sense? And how does

---

[60] "I am resolved," "we are resolved," to what? Sometimes we do not know. We are resolute in "something," resolved to "do something," without knowing why but without losing any of the strength and intensity of a "resolution" that stands as itself, in the words, in 1921, in the texts of "revolutionary syndicalist committees" of the French CGT (see Colson, 1986: 104), but thus mobilizing considerable forces, struggling body and effects all the more unpredictable: it is first a "resolution" with no strings attached or definite object.

[61] In French, "trop d'impôt tue l'impôt," a neoliberal economic slogan. Here, the sense of the phrase is to stand for the assumption of a self-annihilating plurality, a kind of marketplace in which all the differences cancel one another out. [Translator's note.]

this take place below the level of the mechanical logorrhea that comprises everyday speech or the constant flow of ideas (or moods) that assail us, passing from one into another, merging, transforming, diverging, etc.? The problem for Lacan, but also for all of the structuralists, is knitted into a thesis. For Lacan, the signifier and signified are barred from one another (see Figures 1 and 2). Incommensurable, like Heaven and Earth in the old monotheisms (Figure 3), they tend to operate independently of one another and on their own accounts, with the signifiers on top, structured by language and its erratic effects, thinking for us, guiding our actions and our wills. On the bottom, or below, we find confused and constantly changing states of consciousness, as in dreams.

This disproportion between the hierarchy of top and bottom, between Heaven and Earth (we leave here the interesting question of Hell), but also between thought and extension, the symbolic and the real, etc., is nothing very new. Historically, it has given rise to a variety of solutions. For example, monotheism, with its single temple and divine revelation, spatially and historically situated (the *high places* of the Bible), in opposition to the proliferation of polytheist and animist meeting points, attempts to impose a monopoly of communication in the form of the temple of Jerusalem, Rome, or Mecca, and especially the single Book (see Figures 4 and 5). Or more recently, on the terrain of philosophy alone, where Descartes situates the point of intersection (between thought and extension) in the philosophico-anatomical *high place* that is the pineal gland (Figure 6).[62]

The apparently more limited question Lacan poses is therefore constructed within an old problem which he formulates in modern terms, as follows: how can the flow of signifiers, the sequence of words and phrases, be knitted onto the flow of signifieds (ideas or "states of consciousness," for example)? How can quilting points be formed, these "high places" where Earth and Heaven, but also signifier and signified, or the symbolic and the real, are knit together and take shape, not in Mecca or in the temple in Jerusalem but in those other chapels that are psychoanalysts' offices? How can high and low bend, curve towards one another and form nodes [*nœuds*] of meaning? Here, Lacan lets us make three points of particular interest for libertarian thought.

> 1 — The first point, actually quite comforting: it is true that the way the signifier and the signified always tend to slide over one another, hanging together with real difficulty, has something of the exceptional and problematic if not impossible character of the encounter between Heaven and Earth. We can observe, however, that this lack of attachment is especially noticeable and evident in psychoanalytic treatment, in particular the couch itself, the story of dreams, verbal associations, etc. In real life, the signifiers uttered and the states of consciousness signified may well brush up against one another. They are mostly found within practical situations that always force them to be knitted to one another, to acquire meaning

---

[62] One could also place Lacan's "Borromean knot" here.

and substance within these situations.[63] Let us take an example. If, while driving, someone said: "look at that big *bahut* [truck] on the right!" We understand as soon as the *bahut* in question has nothing to do with the *bahut* [sideboard] where our grandmother arranged the jams that we stole when we were little, before we went to a boarding school where there was no jam, then had recurrent distressing dreams in which the *bahut* [sideboard] turns into a *dahut* [goat-monster] and an exhausting chase, etc. Ordinary life, the most commonplace, therefore, determines the moments and meanings, and thus knits together signifiers and signifieds, not in the manner of the sociologist who could identify their frameworks or grammars of action, but through a tangle of particular situations, issues, stances, sketches, statements that are more or less implicit and chaotic, even in the moments that are seemingly the most structured and repetitive, as when the priest, saying, "I baptize you in the name of the Father, the Son, and the Holy Ghost" seeks to knit the signifier and signified together in a clear and unambiguous way. And it is here, from an anarchist perspective, that Lacan's analysis is suddenly of great interest. In this analysis, psychoanalysis and everyday life tend to present the two extremes of how signifiers and signifieds come to be knitted together. On the one hand, there are the prophecies of the couch where signifiers and signifieds slide freely over one another, with only a few sporadic attachments where Lacan apprehends what he calls the "quilting point" (the moment when he charged for the consultation). On the other hand, we find those ordinary situations in which it is rather the anarchic excess of attachments between signifiers and signifieds, the infinite number of concomitant, potential, or possible knots [*nœuds*] which, by their excessiveness, make the knots [*nœuds*] of the quilting points problematic. If the meaning and the actual deployment of entities pose a real problem, it is twofold or in the direction of two extremes: lack and scarcity in the one case, oversupply and excess in the other, in those ordinary situations where, as Bergson says about the pragmatism of William James, there is always "too much of this, too much of that, too much of everything" – too many notes, as Salieri said of Mozart's music, too many waves and drops of water making their singular voices heard, which thus seem to prevent us from hearing the sound of the sea (see Figures 7 and 8) (Bergson, [1934] 2002: 267-8). In short, psychoanalytic treatment, in the rarified atmosphere of its laboratory, reveals what is masked, paradoxically, by the chaotic abundance of real life: namely, the problematic nature of beings, of their freedom and their association, and through this, the no less problematic relationship between signifiers and signifieds, where they are knitted together in the form of the quilting points.

2 — But as an exception to the rule (by virtue of its rarity), analytic treatment provides a second indication of how to grasp the anarchy of the real and how it knits together signifier and signified. Theoretically, the

---

[63] In spite of all the misunderstandings and mistaken identities that comprise the charm and the bother of daily life.

Lacanian quilting point is a game of language, that language which operates in psychoanalytic treatment. Without going into details one can say that the quilting point is related to the sentence, the fact that the sentences form an entity in which the ending, the poorly named *dénouement*, is (first) to knit [*nouer*] the words preceding this conclusion, giving them a sense of unity, in retrospect, one might say, as when we reach the end of a movie or a thriller, when Hercule Poirot, usually in a crowded room and in the presence of all the protagonists, "tidies up" the confusion of events and gives the characters (and readers) their meaning and thus the real dramatic unity of the up until now disparate elements of the story that you have just read, the "key to the mystery," the "last word," as they say.[64] We will return to the importance (from an anarchist point of view) of the times and becomings that accompany history and stories, but for now we can see how, in the analytical situation, the quilting point, this conclusion that gives meaning, in retrospect, is not only a game of language. Through the utterance of the patient, it involves something else, two essential realities: *desire* and the *subject*, or to put it in anarchist or Proudhonian terms, *force* and *subjectivity*, the *real* and *individuation* thought as subjectivity, as a point of subjectivation. This aspect of Lacan's analysis is very interesting because in its particular place, it reveals (perhaps) not only the *subjective* (and phantasmic) dimension of lived experiences in ordinary situations, but the very nature of these situations, which it is no longer appropriate to think in the constraining form of external and objective *frameworks*, homologous to the science that claims to seize them, but as pure events and through subjective experience and where managers do experience that one where external determinism turns into inner determination, where the (logical) "resolution" of a problem declares the intensity of an entirely internal "resolution" or "will." Thanks to the Lacanian model, the desert of the cure is peopled with the superabundance and thus the anarchy of the events of ordinary life, a multitude of quilting points, wild in a sense, but all functioning, even in the chaos of their diversity, on the model of the rare and precious associative and subjective closures of analytic treatment. Consequently, any entity existing at a given time, and there are many – whether human or not human, social, physical, linguistic, spiritual or land-based, pervasive or only potential long-term or fleeting, microscopic or at the scale of the entire world – can be traced back to desires or forces, to subjects or singular subjectivities. This hypothesis may seem strange, in view of the narrow horizons of psychoanalysis, but it is at the very heart of Proudhon's thought or Tarde's, for example, and of course that of many other thinkers: Spinoza, Whitehead, Benjamin, Deleuze, Foucault, and so on. In short, one could say that the Lacanian quilting point contributes to voicing that reality and its anarchic abundance, the unceasing agitation of an infinite number of evanescent and ephemeral beings, but with all the equally infinite force and desire that then maintain their existence, an anarchic and thoroughly subjective reality that defies any illusion of objectivity – e.g., the objectivity

---

[64] Which thus *stitches* everything up [*noue*] even as it *unravels* the mystery [*dénoue*].

91

of science, a quilting point like any other, only slightly more pretentious than the others, a quilting point that does not know itself as such, that is likewise unconscious of the imperialist character of its *will to know*, of its own desire.[65]

3 — Lacan makes a third and final remark about the quilting point, something that also concerns libertarian thought and the exact point where Lacanian theory and its structuralist background, however, seem most remote from anarchism: the question of time, duration and history. In libertarian thought, the real (that which is) consists of an infinite number of subjective, fleeting and discontinuous entities in a constant state of transformation; the duration and becoming, the histories and stories of these entities, their births and deaths, their encounters and their transformations, are therefore an essential part of anarchist ontology. For anarchism, everything is history [*histoire*] (in the sense that one *tells stories* [*fait des histoires*]); everything is duration and becoming, an infinite and anarchic multitude of durations and becomings.

By contrast, Lacan, as a structuralist of strict observance, tends to radically reject duration and time in his consideration of the human psyche and, more generally, of the symbolic which is supposed to serve as the matrix and framework for the human world. On the terrain of sociology and history, we find Althusser in this position, for example, in his haughty and lasting denunciation of historicism and empiricism. For structuralism, human realities can only be taken into account in a synchronic, timeless manner. Obviously, Lacan is not unaware that duration, becoming, and time exist, if only via the blood and fluids of birth, sex, and death. But this duration, this becoming, and this time exist only on the side of things, and thus on the side of the signifieds and their flux, largely inaccessible (and, for Lacan, terrifying). It is found on the side of reality, but reality is barred to humans. Human beings are condemned to perceive the world and thus themselves only through the paltry dimension of the symbolic, with its radically synchronic and repetitive character.[66] The signifying chain which, on the terrain of the symbolic, orders mental life and human interaction, does have its own temporality. But that time is radically different from the duration and becoming of things. Lacan defines the temporality of the symbolic and thus the signifier in a particularly illuminating way. He calls it "*logical time*." The concept of logical time (of the repetition of the same) is in no way specifically Lacanian. It lies at the heart of the presuppositions of science and thus at the heart of the human sciences when they claim to be

---

[65] On the particularly deadly nature of this desire or will, in addition to Foucault, see Georges Bernanos, especially the character of "monsieur Ouine" (2000) or even Saint-Marin and the parish priest of Luzarnes in *Under Satan's Sun* (2001).

[66] On Lacan's inability (or refusal), unlike Althusser, to recognize in the "real" a "function" that is not "negative," belonging to "an impossible or a traumatic event that is unrepresentable" see Balibar (2014: xvii). On the problematic nature of Lacan's relations to the physical realities of birth and death, see Marini [1986] (1992).

scientific. It is found for example in Durkheimian positivism, or in the approaches in terms of *frames of experience* (or the *grammars* of a certain pragmatism) in which, as Lacan says, we find "the battery of signifiers [...] [that] are already there" (Lacan, 2006: 13). As Lacan says: "one's bearings are already laid down, the signifying reference-points of the problem are already marked in it and the solution will never go beyond them" (Lacan, 1998: 40). Logical time is also found in historiography, not only or even primarily in the structuralist historiography of the *Annales* school, but in the more traditional chronological historiography, that storytelling [*histoire*] so improperly called the *history of events* [*histoire événementielle*], a history based on the logical chain of causes and effects, in which chronology, determinism, and narrative form such a solid *ménage* (*à trois*). So, in summary, we can say that for Lacan, the logical time of the signifying chain, as the basis of representations and human actions, does not open onto the duration of things. This access to it is barred, except at precisely one site: the quilting point. And it is there that everything changes.

We can summarize Lacan's thesis or intuition as follows: the quilting point reinjects the duration of things into logical time (thus, that of the physicists, the historians, and the sociologists). Lacan explains how the quilting point, because it is the place of desire and human subjectivity, has a "diachronic function" (Lacan, 2002: 292) The quilting point corresponds to "a movement of the subject that opens up only to close again in a certain temporal *pulsation*" (Lacan, 1998: 125; my emphasis). But Lacan goes further. He added: "[this] *pulsation* I regard as being more radical than the insertion in the signifier that no doubt motivates it, but is not primary to it at the level of essence" (Lacan, 1975: 274). For Lacan, what is taking place thus has something to do with desire and subjectivity, but also with things and their duration. Reintroduced into the heart of human existence, i.e., into its subjectivity, its lived reality, and its desire, the duration of things is prior to any signifier. Human subjectivity still ultimately depends on the signifier and on logical time, but very weakly and not without contradiction, since Lacan reduces this dependence to a simple and vague "motivation" preceded by a skeptical (and rather pregnant) "probably" (Lacan, 1998: 128).

Let us recall what we have observed so far. The quilting point as a place of subjectivity and desire, caught up in the duration of things, appears within the analytic cure. It even constitutes an essential moment in this process, albeit a rare moment. The relationship between signifier and signified is not as barred as Lacan would like to think. Let us recognize its rarity – but with a new reservation that changes everything. The quilting point is rare, but only in the particular situation of the analytic cure, or in dreams. In reality, however, it is extremely common (too common, actually). It is singular each time, albeit in the sense of Benjamin's remark that *the exception is the rule* (Benjamin, 1986: 3, 433; 1986: 257). The quilting point and subjectivity, desire and the time that attach to them, are always exceptional, odd things, but as an infinite number of exceptions, they become the (admittedly chaotic) rule of human existence, as of everything.

Through the image of the quilting points (drawn from the domain of handicraft), Lacan helps us to grasp the way in which Proudhon theorizes the anarchy of beings. Lacan also allows us to see how this anarchy is in no way incompatible with Proudhon's Franche-Comtois character – an obstinacy and stubbornness demonstrated, to varying degrees, by all possible beings. As a "focal point where all the relations of things are reflected and combined," "like the plant and the crystal, but to a greater degree than these" (Proudhon, [1858] 1935: 3, 162; [1853] 1946: 64), the individual, whether resolved or irresolute, is both an event and a quilting point, a high place, able to knit together and bring into focus not only heaven and earth, the signifier and the signified, or even the hierarchy of the two Cartesian substances, but an infinite number of planes, perspectives, and *raisons d'être* that deprive it of any essential identity in their constant transformation, and at the same time, help explain its astonishing capacity to persist in being.

Figures

Figure 1:

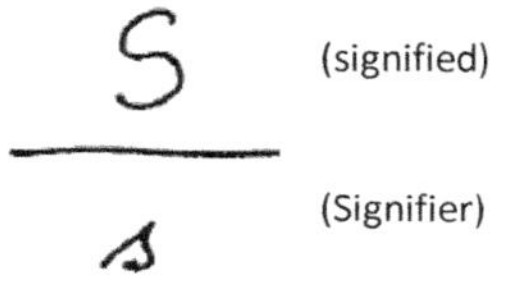

$$\frac{S}{\text{\textit{s}}}$$

S   (signified)

s   (Signifier)

Figure 2:

$$\frac{S - S - S - S - S}{s - s - s - s - s}$$

S – S – S – S – S   (Flow or chain of signifiers)

s – s – s – s – s   (Flow or chain of signifieds)

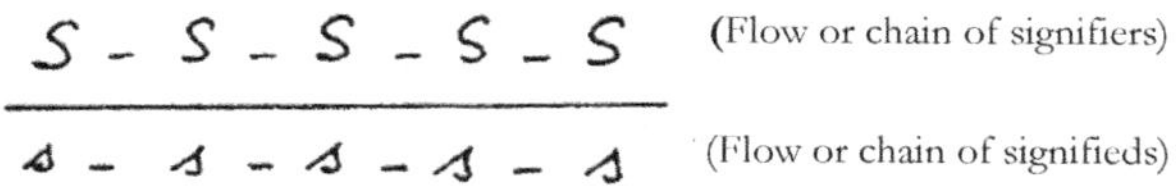

Figure 3:

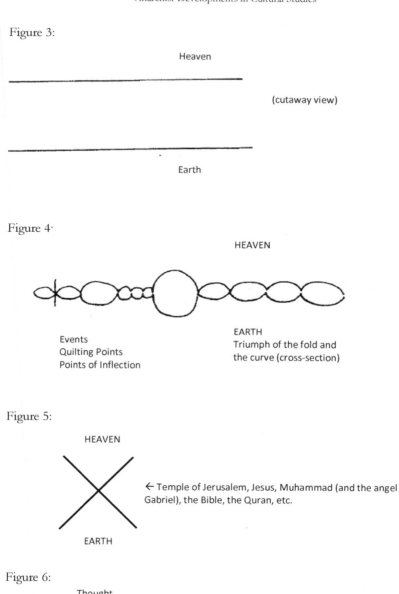

Heaven

(cutaway view)

Earth

Figure 4·

HEAVEN

Events
Quilting Points
Points of Inflection

EARTH
Triumph of the fold and
the curve (cross-section)

Figure 5:

HEAVEN

← Temple of Jerusalem, Jesus, Muhammad (and the angel
Gabriel), the Bible, the Quran, etc.

EARTH

Figure 6:

Thought
Spirit
Soul

← Pineal gland

Body
Matter
Extension

Figure 7:

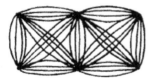

Mechanical quilting points, organized
by the frameworks of experience
(seen from above).

Partial, but exhaustive in their
repetition of the same.

Figure 8:

Anarchic (and real) quilting points (again, seen
from above). A mere selection of the surface,
from a certain angle, from any point in the
universe.

References

Balibar, Etienne. (2014) "Althusser and the 'Ideological State Apparatuses'" (G.M. Goshgarian, Trans.), in Louis Althusser, *On the Reproduction of Capitalism: Ideology and Ideological State Apparatuses*. London: Verso. vii-xviii.

Benjamin, Walter. (1986) "On the Concept of History," *Illuminations* (Hannah Arendt, Ed., Harry Zohn, Trans.), New York: Schocken Books.

Bergson, Henri. [1934] (2002) "On the Pragmatism of William James: Truth and Reality" (Melissa McMahon, Trans.), in *Henri Bergson: Key Writings* (Keith Ansell Pearson, Ed.), New York: Continuum.

Bernanos, Georges. (2000) *Monsieur Ouine* (William Bush, Trans.). Lincoln: University of Nebraska Press.

Bernanos, Georges. (2001) *Under Satan's Sun* (J. C. Whitehouse, Trans.). Lincoln: University of Nebraska Press.

Colson, Daniel. (2010) "Éclectisme et dimension autodidacte de l'anarchisme ouvrier," in *Figures du maître ignorant: savoir et emancipation* (Marc Derycke & Michel Péroni, Eds.), Saint-Etienne, France: Université de Saint-Etienne.

Colson, Daniel. (2007) "Proudhon, Lacan, et les points de capiton." *Contr'Un*, Vol. 1: 106-15.

Colson, Daniel. (2007) "Anarchist Readings of Spinoza" (Jesse Cohn & Nathan Jun, Trans.), *Journal of French Philosophy*, Vol. 17, No. 2: 90-129.

Colson, Daniel. (2001) *Petit lexique philosophique de l'anarchisme de Proudhon à Deleuze*. Paris: Librairie Générale Française.

Colson, Daniel. (1986) *Anarcho-syndicalisme et communisme, Saint-Etienne (1920-1925)*. Saint-Etienne: Centre d'études forézienne, 1986.

Deleuze, Gilles. (1995) *Negotiations, 1972-1990* (Martin Joughin, Trans.). New York: Columbia University Press.

Deleuze, Gilles., & Guattari, Félix. (1980) *A Thousand Plateaus: Capitalism and Schizophrenia* (Brian Massumi, Trans.). London: Continuum.

Johnston, Adrian. (2005) *Time Driven: Metapsychology and the Splitting of the Drive*. Evanston, Ill: Northwestern University Press.

Koch, Andrew M. (1993) "Poststructuralism and the Epistemological Basis of Anarchism," *Philosophy of the Social Sciences*, Vol. 23, No. 3, (Sept): 327-351.

Lacan, Jacques. (1978) *The Seminar of Jacques Lacan, Book II: The Ego in Freud's Theory and in the Technique of Psychoanalysis, 1954-1955* (Sylvana Tomaselli, Trans.). New York: W.W. Norton & Co..

Lacan, Jacques. (1975) *The Language of the Self: The Function of Language in Psychoanalysis*, (Anthony Wilden, Trans.). New York: Dell Pub. Co.

Lacan, Jacques. (1998) *The Seminar of Jacques Lacan, Book XI: The Four Fundamental Concepts of Psychoanalysis* (Alan Sheridan, Trans., Jacques-Alain Miller, Ed.). New York: W. W. Norton & Co.

Lacan, Jacques. (2002) *Ecrits: A Selection*. New York: W.W. Norton & Co.

Lacan, Jacques. (2006) *The Seminar of Jacques Lacan, Book XVII: The Other Side of Psychoanalysis* (Russell Grigg, Trans.). New York: W.W. Norton & Co.

Marx, Karl. [1847] (1995) *The Poverty of Philosophy* (H. Quelch, Trans.). Amherst: Prometheus Books.

May, Todd. (2002) "Lacanian Anarchism and the Left," *Theory & Event* Vol. 6, No. 1.

Proudhon, Pierre-Joseph. [1858] (1935) *De la Justice dans la Révolution et dans l'Eglise* (Célestin Charles Alfred Bouglé and Henri Moysset, Eds.). Paris: Rivière.

Proudhon, Pierre-Joseph. [1853] (1946) *Philosophie du progrès* (Célestin Charles Alfred Bouglé and Henri Moysset, Eds.). Paris: M. Rivière.

Proudhon, Pierre-Joseph. (1983) *Mémoires sur ma vie* (Bernard Voyenne, Ed.). Paris: Maspero.

Proudhon, Pierre-Joseph. [1846] (2011) *System of Economic Contradictions [or, The Philosophy of Poverty]* (Benjamin R. Tucker, Clarence L. Swartz, and Shawn Wilbur, Trans.), in *Property Is Theft!: A Pierre-Joseph Proudhon Anthology* (Iain McKay, Ed.). Oakland: AK Press. 167-256.

Pouget, Émile. (2003) *Direct Action* (Kate Sharpley Library, Trans.). London: Kate Sharpley Library.

Robinson, Andrew. (2005) "The Political Theory of Constitutive Lack: A Critique," *Theory & Event Vol.* 8, No. 1.

de Seixas, Jacy Alvez. (1989) *Mémoire et oubli, Anarchisme et syndicalisme révolutionnaire au Brésil*, Paris: Editions de la Maison des sciences de l'homme.

Tarde, Gabriel. (2011) *Monadology and Sociology* (Theo Lorenc, Trans.) Prahran, Vic: re.press

Hurchalla, George (2016) *Going Underground: American Punk 1979 - 1989*. PM Press: Oakland, California.

On 14 January 1978, The Sex Pistols played the final show of their first North American tour at the Winterlands in San Francisco. For George Hurchalla, this show is important not only because it symbolizes the passing of the torch, Virgin Records to SST, England to the United States, commercial success to thriving underground scene. No, he instead brings together punk's many definitions – a shared identity, genre of popular music, and sense of fashion – in order to work through punk's multiple meanings. The Winterlands show thus marks the exact historical moment where and when he begins his social history of the American do-it-yourself (DIY) punk scene. In lieu of highlighting punk's "aboveground" major label successes (e.g., Sex Pistols, The Ramones, and The Clash), Hurchalla fixates on the American "underground" (11), or what he and others call the DIY scene.

However the second edition of *Going Underground: American Punk 1979 - 1989* extends DIY punk and its histories past Dischord Records, Black Flag, and the early 1980s Washington, DC and Los Angeles scenes. Many of the book's 29 chapters revolve around creating a more readily-available archive that anthologizes some of lesser-known scenes, venues and bands, such as Miami, Florida, Club Doobee in East Lansing, or Sluggo from Cincinnati. The thorough analysis complements the author's own punk coming-of-age with zines, interviews, and flyers from different scenes – big city and small towns – all across the country, not to mention a number of never-before-seen photographs that give face to the voices of punk's DIY past. But *Going Underground* does not stop here; it berates punk's ultimate antagonist, Ronald Reagan, without losing sight of the fact that the DIY ethos is "rugged individualism" *par excellence*. While Reagan's real supporters were a "herd of mindless sheep," DIY punks for Hurchalla were the "actual rugged individualists" because they "took the necessary steps to have [their] voices heard" (104). Besides, Ian MacKaye, one of the founders of Dischord Records, reminds us elsewhere just how much work and time are used up by the DIY mode of production. As Reagan set in motion a world where instead of relying on the state for handouts, people learned to pull themselves up by their own bootstraps; MacKaye and countless other punks refused to be held hostage by the demands of the music industry, so in response they created their own scene wherein they make the rules – by punks, for punks.

Hurchalla wisely extends the American DIY punk scene past 1981 and beyond the coasts in space, though his point would be more effective if he did not severely overlook the many contributions of women. Sure, the names of many female punks are mentioned sporadically throughout (e.g. Philadelphia's Nancy Petriello Barile, Black Flag's Kira Roessler, and Sue Harshe of the Meat Puppets), but their purpose serves only as a means to connect various male-dominated scenes and bands. Indeed, towards the end, Hurchalla, in what can only be described as a tokenistic addendum, includes the chapter "Pardon Me, I'm Only Bleeding" (337-50) which opens with discussion of women in the scene. And yet, it still only devotes about a third (approximately 4 pages) to the experiences of women in western punk scenes, from Los Angeles to San Francisco, Portland and Seattle. Although its clever title references a popular Butthole Surfers song, its contents again leave a lot to be desired. Rather than placing the contributions of women within the chapters relevant to those scenes, Hurchalla isolates their experiences; which, as a result, implies that women are not fully integrated into the scenes he examines. He cannot in good faith claim to write an inclusive social history of the American DIY punk scene that isn't more indebted to the contributions of women.

Ultimately, Hurchalla fills in the blank spots on the punk map by documenting some of the lesser known scenes, yet his way of bringing these histories to new life raise a number of concerns. Since the book is shaped by personal experience, Hurchalla over-emphasizes his own story at the expense of others. As such, *Going Underground: American Punk 1979 - 1989* successfully undoes punk's diversity when readers shouldn't have to put their ear to the ground in order to learn about some of the names, faces, and bands that existed parallel to the author's own frame of reference. Even so, the book joins a growing list of punk titles published by PM Press. *Going Underground* represents a commendable attempt to lessen the gap between 1980s cultural historian and punk newcomer, but I'm not entirely convinced that it lives up to its very un-DIY, $21.95 price tag.

Corey Ponder
Trent University

Made in the USA
Las Vegas, NV
26 February 2022

44628786R00059